# Social Networking for the Over 50s

**Prentice Hall**
is an imprint of

Harlow, England • London • New York • Boston • San Francisco • Toronto • Sydney • Singapore • Hong Kong
Tokyo • Seoul • Taipei • New Delhi • Cape Town • Madrid • Mexico City • Amsterdam • Munich • Paris • Milan

**PEARSON EDUCATION LIMITED**

Edinburgh Gate
Harlow CM20 2JE
Tel: +44 (0)1279 623623
Fax: +44 (0)1279 431059
Website: www.pearsoned.co.uk

First published in Great Britain in 2012

Pearson Education is not responsible for the content of third-party internet sites.

ISBN: 978-0-273-76107-5

British Library Cataloguing-in-Publication Data
A catalogue record for this book is available from the British Library

Library of Congress Cataloging-in-Publication Data
Myer, Tom.
  Social networking for the over 50s in simple steps / Thomas Myer.
    p. cm.
  ISBN 978-0-273-76107-5 (pbk.)
1. Online social networks. 2. Internet and older people. I. Title.
  HM742.M94 2012
  004.67'80846--dc23
                                                2011041564

10 9 8 7 6 5 4 3 2 1
15 14 13 12 11

Designed by pentacorbig, High Wycombe
Typeset in 11/14pt ITC Stone Sans by 3
Printed and bound in Great Britain by Scotprint, Haddington, East Lothian

# Social Networking
# for the Over 50s

in Simple
steps

Thomas Myer

# Use your computer with confidence

Get to grips with practical computing tasks with minimal time, fuss and bother.

*In Simple Steps guides* guarantee immediate results. They tell you everything you need to know on a specific application; from the most essential tasks to master, to every activity you'll want to accomplish, through to solving the most common problems you'll encounter.

## Helpful features

To build your confidence and help you to get the most out of your iPad, practical hints, tips and shortcuts feature on every page:

**ALERT:** Explains and provides practical solutions to the most commonly encountered problems

**HOT TIP:** Time and effort saving shortcuts

**SEE ALSO:** Points you to other related tasks and information

**DID YOU KNOW?** Additional features to explore

**WHAT DOES THIS MEAN?**
Jargon and technical terms explained in plain English

## Practical. Simple. Fast.

in Simple steps

# Publisher acknowledgements

We are grateful to the following for permission to reproduce copyright material:

**Figure**
Figure on page 16 from http://www.emarketer.com/Article.aspx?R=1007908, with permission from eMarketer; Figure on page 17 from Image Source Ltd.

**Table**
Table on page 15 from http://www.clickymedia.co.uk/2009/08/uk-facebook-user-statistics-august-2009/, with permission from Clicky Media Ltd.

**Screenshots**
Screenshots on pages 2, 3, 4, 5, 21, 29, 30, 33, 34, 35, 36, 40 and 215 from Twitter, Inc., on pages 6, 7, 8, 9, 19, 23, 25, 43, 44, 45, 46, 47, 48, 49, 50, 51, 52, 53, 54, 55, 59, 60, 61, 62, 63, 64, 65, 66, 67, 68, 69, 70, 183 and 198 from Facebook Inc., on pages 10, 22, 100 and 102 from Tumblr, Inc.; on pages 12, 73, 74, 75, 76, 77, 78, 79, 80, 81, 82, 83, 84, 85, 86, 87, 88, 89, 90, 91, 92, 97, 98, 105, 106, 107, 108, 109 and 184 from Google, Inc.; on page 48 with permission from Amy Sue Anderson; on page 51 with permission from Jennifer Cunningham, Chris Carter and Elizabeth Quintanilla; on page 59 with permission from Noah Masterson, Amy Gelfand and Claire England; on pages 62 and 138 with permission from Stephanie Wonderlin; on page 63 with permission from Stephanie Wonderlin, Stephen Finos and Stephanie Mitchell Carney; on pages 88 and 125 from Hope Doty; on page 95 from *The Guardian*, copyright Guardian News & Media Ltd 2011; on pages 103 and 104 from Posterous, Inc.; on pages 110, 111 and 112 from WordPress; on pages 114, 115, 116, 117, 118, 119, 120, 121, 122, 123, 124, 125 and 126 from Flickr, reproduced with permission of Yahoo! Inc. © 2011 Yahoo! Inc. YAHOO!, the YAHOO! logo, FLICKR and the FLICKR logo are registered trademarks of Yahoo! Inc.; on pages 127, 128, 129, 130 and 131 from Instagram; on page 128 also with permission from Aaron Strout; on pages 132, 133, 134, 135, 136, 137 and 138 from YouTube, LLC; on pages 139, 140, 141, 142, 143 and 144 from Vimeo, LLC; on pages 147, 148, 149, 150, 151 and 152 from Last. fm Limited; on pages 161, 162 and 168 from Spotify; on page 172 with permission from Simon Salt; on pages 174, 175, 176, 177 and 178 from Gowalla, Inc.; on page 187 from DailyBooth, Inc.; on page 188 from AVOS Systems, Inc.; on page 190 from Friends Reunited; on page 192 from Hotlist.com; on page 193 from TravBuddy; on page 194 from Yelp! Inc.; on page 199 from Veign, LLC; on page 206 from Twibes; on page 209 from West Kent Book Club.

In some instances we have been unable to trace the owners of copyright material, and we would appreciate any information that would enable us to do so.

in Simple steps

# Contents at a glance

Top 10 Social Networking
Tips for the Over 50s

## 1 Getting started with social media

- Who uses social media? 15
- Finding your friends and colleagues on social media 19
- Using social media to meet new friends 21
- Using social media to promote a business 24

## 2 Twitter

- Set up a Twitter account 29
- Tweet! 30
- Use a Twitter hashtag 32
- Using Twitter search 36

## 3 Facebook basics

- Set up a Facebook account 43
- Adding a bio 44
- Uploading a profile picture 45
- Finding friends on Facebook 46

## 4 Advanced Facebook

- Asking a question on Facebook 61
- Posting to someone's wall 62
- Tagging someone in a post or a comment 63
- Sending a private message 64

## 5 Google+

- Getting to know Google+ 73
- Sharing on Google+ 74
- Notifications in Google+ 86
- Viewing your own profile on Google+ 88

## 6 Blogging

- Starting your own blog 96
- Finding quality blogs 97
- Before you start a blog 99
- Nine ideas for keeping your blog going 101

## 7 Photos and video

- Create a Flickr account 116
- Introduction to Instagram 127
- Signing up for YouTube 134
- Uploading your first video 135

## 8 Music

- Get music recommendations from Last.fm — 149
- Searching for a song on Blip.fm — 159
- Getting a Spotify account — 162
- Creating and sharing playlists on Spotify — 169

## 9 Location-based services

- Checking in to a location — 176
- Introduction to Foursquare — 179
- Using Facebook check-ins — 183
- Using Google+ check-ins — 184

## 10 Fun social websites to try out

- DailyBooth — 187
- Delicious — 188
- Flixster — 189
- Friends Reunited — 190
- GoodReads — 191
- The Hotlist — 192
- TravBuddy — 193
- Yelp — 194
- DailyMile — 195
- Ravelry — 196

**Top 10 Social Networking Problems Solved**

# Contents

## Top 10 Social Networking Tips for the Over 50s

| | | |
|---|---|---|
| 1 | Set up a Twitter account | 2 |
| 2 | Tweet! | 3 |
| 3 | Tweet a reply to a specific person | 4 |
| 4 | Use a Twitter hashtag | 5 |
| 5 | Set up a Facebook account | 6 |
| 6 | Share what you're doing on Facebook | 7 |
| 7 | Share photos on Facebook | 8 |
| 8 | Share videos on Facebook | 9 |
| 9 | Start blogging with Tumblr | 10 |
| 10 | Introduction to Google+ | 12 |

## 1 Getting started with social media

| | |
|---|---|
| Who uses social media? | 15 |
| Why participate in social media? | 16 |
| Is social media 'viral'? | 17 |
| Privacy and security concerns | 18 |
| Finding your friends and colleagues on social media | 19 |
| Using social media to meet new friends | 21 |
| Using social media to follow a hobby or passion | 22 |
| Using social media to organise people for a cause or movement | 23 |
| Using social media to promote a business | 24 |

## 2 Twitter

| | |
|---|---|
| Set up a Twitter account | 29 |
| Tweet! | 30 |

● Tweet a reply to a specific person     31

● Use a Twitter hashtag     32

● Finding friends on Twitter     33

● Using Twitter search     36

● Sending a direct message     37

● Installing Tweetdeck     38

● Using Twitter on an iPhone     40

## 3 Facebook basics

● Set up a Facebook account     43

● Adding a bio     44

● Uploading a profile picture     45

● Finding friends on Facebook     46

● Share what you're doing on Facebook     47

● Adding a comment to a friend's Facebook status     48

● Viewing a friend's profile     49

● Friending someone on Facebook     50

● Liking on Facebook     51

● Share photos on Facebook     52

● Share videos on Facebook     53

● Share links on Facebook     54

● Tagging people on Facebook     55

## 4 Advanced Facebook

● Using the notes feature to 'blog' on Facebook     59

● Asking a question on Facebook     61

● Posting to someone's wall     62

● Tagging someone in a post or a comment     63

● Sending a private message     64

Creating an event on Facebook                          66

Liking a fan page                                      68

Telling others about a fan page                        69

Facebook on your iPhone                                70

# 5 Google+

Getting to know Google+                                73

Sharing on Google+                                     74

Sharing a photo on Google+                             75

Sharing a photo album on Google+                       76

Viewing photos from your circle on Google+             77

Sharing a video on Google+                             78

Adding comments on Google+                             79

Adding a +1 on Google+                                 80

Muting a post on Google+                               81

Sharing on Google+                                     82

Restrict sharing on Google+                            83

Working with circles in Google+                        84

Notifications in Google+                               86

Viewing a specific stream on Google+                   87

Viewing your own profile on Google+                    88

Starting a hangout on Google+                          89

Sparks on Google+                                      90

Your Google+ settings                                  92

# 6 Blogging

Starting your own blog                                 96

Finding quality blogs                                  97

Before you start a blog                                99

● Nine ideas for keeping your blog going     101

● Start blogging with Tumblr     102

● Start blogging with Posterous     103

● Start blogging with Blogger     105

● Start blogging with WordPress.com     110

## 7 Photos and video

● Introduction to Flickr     115

● Create a Flickr account     116

● Upload an image to Flickr     117

● Organise images into sets     119

● Search for images     124

● Connect with people on Flickr     126

● Introduction to Instagram     127

● Downloading the application     128

● Taking a picture with Instagram     129

● Finding friends on Instagram     131

● Introduction to YouTube     132

● Searching for and watching videos on YouTube     133

● Signing up for YouTube     134

● Uploading your first video     135

● Subscribing to a channel on YouTube     138

● Introduction to Vimeo     139

● Signing up for Vimeo     140

● Uploading a video     142

● Exploring Vimeo     143

## 8 Music

● Introduction to Last.fm     147

Starting a Last.fm profile    148

Get music recommendations from Last.fm    149

Downloading the Last.fm Scrobbler    150

Adding favourite artists to Last.fm manually    152

Listening to music on Last.fm    154

Seeing recommended music on Last.fm    155

Introduction to Blip.fm    157

Signing up for Blip.fm    158

Searching for a song on Blip.fm    159

Blipping a song    160

Introduction to Spotify    161

Getting a Spotify account    162

Installing Spotify    163

Importing your music to Spotify    164

Playing a song on Spotify    165

Seeing an artist's playlist    166

Seeing all songs on an album    167

Starring songs    168

Creating and sharing playlists on Spotify    169

Finding Facebook friends on Spotify    171

## 9 Location-based services

Downloading Gowalla    175

Checking in to a location    176

About Me in Gowalla    177

Finding friends on Gowalla    178

Introduction to Foursquare    179

Downloading the app    180

Checking in to a location    181

- Using Foursquare to explore    182
- Using Facebook check-ins    183
- Using Google+ check-ins    184

## 10 Fun social websites to try out

- DailyBooth    187
- Delicious    188
- Flixster    189
- Friends Reunited    190
- GoodReads    191
- The Hotlist    192
- TravBuddy    193
- Yelp    194
- DailyMile    195
- Ravelry    196

## Top 10 Social Networking Problems Solved

1 Privacy issues    198
2 Security issues    199
3 Oversharing    201
4 Inauthenticity    202
5 Friending too many people    204
6 Friending too few people    206
7 Trolls    208
8 Forgetting the social part of social media    209
9 Getting distracted by too much social media    211
10 Not participating enough in social media    213

# Top 10 Social Networking Tips for the Over 50s

| 1 | Set up a Twitter account | 2 |
| 2 | Tweet! | 3 |
| 3 | Tweet a reply to a specific person | 4 |
| 4 | Use a Twitter hashtag | 5 |
| 5 | Set up a Facebook account | 6 |
| 6 | Share what you're doing on Facebook | 7 |
| 7 | Share photos on Facebook | 8 |
| 8 | Share videos on Facebook | 9 |
| 9 | Start blogging with Tumblr | 10 |
| 10 | Introduction to Google+ | 12 |

# Tip 1: Set up a Twitter account

Twitter is one of the fastest-growing services in the social media universe. Setting up an account is very easy. All you have to do is:

**1** Open a web browser and visit http://twitter.com.

**2** Under the headline New to Twitter? you'll find a form.

**3** Fill out your name, email address and a password and click Sign up.

Once you've signed up, start following people who are of interest to you. Twitter will show you a list of featured Twitter users as part of the sign-up process. Don't forget to add a bio and upload an avatar.

If you like, go ahead and follow @myerman (that's me) and say hello!

**ALERT:** You must use a unique email address to get an account on Twitter.

# Tip 2: Tweet!

Now that you're on Twitter, it's time to send out a tweet. A tweet is a Twitter message. Please don't say 'twit' or that you 'twit'. Your message has to be 140 characters or less.

To send out a tweet:

**1** Make sure you're logged into Twitter.

**2** Under What's happening? you'll notice a blank text field. Click that field.

**3** Compose your message, keeping it to 140 characters or less. Most people tell others what they're doing at the moment (reading a book, enjoying the outdoors or going shopping) or share a link or photo.

**4** Once you're happy with your tweet, click the Tweet button.

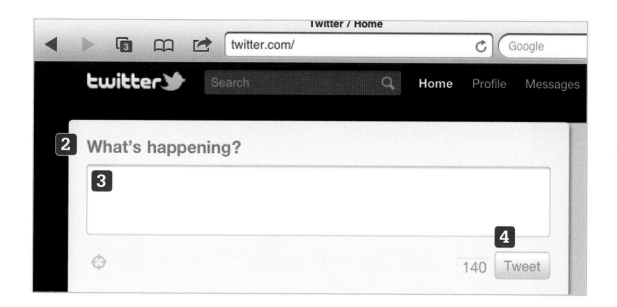

# Tip 3: Tweet a reply to a specific person

Sometimes you don't want to send a message to everyone who is following you, but instead want to send a tweet for someone's attention. You can do this by starting your tweet with the person's @ name (in other words, their twitter handle – mine is @myerman).

To send a reply:

**1** Make sure you're logged into Twitter.

**2** You'll notice a blank text field. Click that field.

**3** Compose your message, keeping it to 140 characters or less. Usually people start a reply with the recipient's @ name, but this isn't necessary.

**4** Once you're happy with your tweet, click the Tweet button.

**twitter** ❥    Search     🔍    **Home**    Profile    Messages

**Mention hopedoty**

**3** | @hopedoty thanks so much for taking care of that!

**4**

📷 ✛       91   Tweet

Timeline    **@Mentions**    Retweets ▾   Searches ▾   Lists ▾

**HOT TIP:** Sending someone an @ reply is still public, and anyone can read it, but putting their @ name in the tweet will increase the likelihood that they will see it, especially if they have a busy timeline.

# Tip 4: Use a Twitter hashtag

Twitter hashtags were invented to help busy Twitter users organise their conversations. In the Twitter world, it's very easy to follow lots of different people with lots of different interests. Although you can use the search functions on Twitter to find out what's interesting to you (for example, you might do a search for 'kayaks' or 'gardening' or 'travel'), different groups will probably have adopted special hashtags for different hobbies, events or topics.

For example, an author who is touring the country and giving lectures might create her own hashtag (#booktour2011, for example), using that hashtag in her tweets. Her fans might also tweet using that hashtag. By searching for that hashtag, you not only get to see what the author is doing, but also meet and interact with a whole bunch of people you might never otherwise have met.

To use a hashtag in your tweets:

**1** Make sure you're logged into Twitter.

**2** You'll notice a blank text field. Click that field.

**3** Compose your message, keeping it to 140 characters or less. Add your hashtag to the tweet wherever you like. Many people put them at the end, but that isn't necessary.

**4** Once you're happy with your tweet, click the Tweet button.

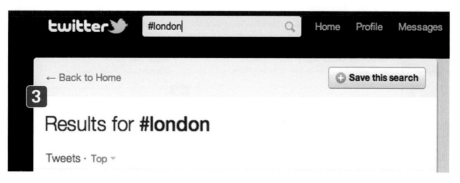

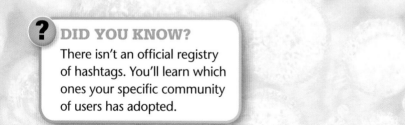

**? DID YOU KNOW?**
There isn't an official registry of hashtags. You'll learn which ones your specific community of users has adopted.

# Tip 5: Set up a Facebook account

Facebook is the most popular social networking site in the world, with 600 million users (and counting) worldwide. You're more likely to run into old school friends, relatives and colleagues on Facebook than on just about any other place.

To set up a Facebook account:

**1** Open a web browser and visit http://www.facebook.com.

**2** Enter your first and last name in the Sign Up form.

**3** Enter your email address, then confirm it.

**4** Enter a password.

**5** Select your gender from the drop-down list.

**6** Enter your birthday (it's used to verify that you are over 18).

**7** Click Sign Up.

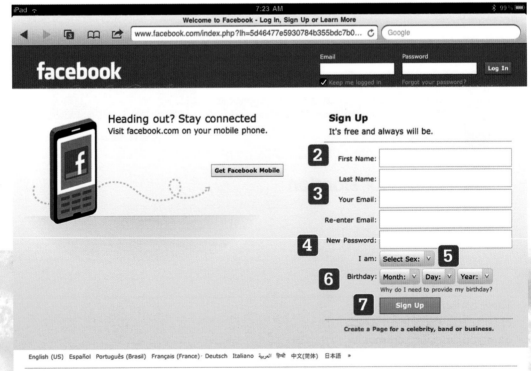

# Tip 6: Share what you're doing on Facebook

Now that you're on Facebook, it's time to tell your friends and family what it is you're up to. Facebook lets you do that with its Share button.

To update your status:

**1** Make sure you're logged on to Facebook.

**2** You'll notice that at the top of the page is a series of options. Click Update Status.

**3** In the Status field is some placeholder text: What's on your mind? Simply click in the status field and replace that text with your own, for example: 'Going to the market today, with any luck I can find some fresh seasonal vegetables there!'

# Tip 7: Share photos on Facebook

Once you're on Facebook, you can share all kinds of interesting news and items with your friends and family. One thing people share a lot of is photos.

To share a photo:

**1** Make sure you're logged into Facebook.

**2** At the very top of the page you'll see Add Photo/Video – click that link.

**3** You then have the option of uploading a photo, taking a photo with your webcam or creating an album with many photos in it. For now, let's upload a photo.

**4** Click Upload a Photo. Click Choose File and then browse through your computer's folders to find the image you want to upload.

**5** You can also add a caption to the photo.

**6** Click Share when you're ready to share this photo with friends.

**2**

| ☰ Update Status  ▣ Add Photo / Video  ☰ Ask Question |

| Upload Photo / Video | Use Webcam | Create Photo Album |

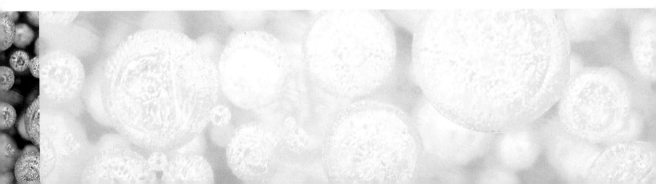

# Tip 8: Share videos on Facebook

More and more of us have easy access to digital video recorders and smartphones with video-recording capabilities. The process of shooting a short video and then sharing it with all your friends on Facebook couldn't be easier:

**1** Make sure you're logged into Facebook.

**2** At the very top of the page you'll see Add Photo/Video. Click that link.

**3** You can record a video with your webcam, or upload a video. For now, let's just upload a video.

**4** Click Upload Photo/Video.

**5** Click Choose File and then browse your hard drive for the video you want to upload.

**6** Add a caption to the video and click Post.

# Tip 9: Start blogging with Tumblr

Lots of people have been talking about blogging these past few years. For the uninitiated, blogging started out as a way for people to create online journals of their hobbies and interests, and has grown into a worldwide phenomenon.

Mind you, blogging isn't just a bunch of people sharing stories about their cats (although there are plenty of people who do!), it also includes some of the world's

top scientific minds sharing their thoughts on physics, journalists providing 'behind-the-scenes' notes on stories you see on the newscasts, athletes sharing their training regimen, and yes, of course, normal everyday people sharing travelogues, recipes and stories about their lives.

When most people think about blogging, they think 'WordPress'. It's true that WordPress is one of the world's most popular blogging platforms, but installing it requires a level of expertise that most people don't have.

A much easier alternative to getting started quickly is to use a service like Tumblr. Tumblr allows you to create a special-interest blog on its servers within minutes.

**HOT TIP:** Once you've got your first blog post up and running, share a link to that blog post on Twitter and Facebook!

To create a Tumblr:

**1** Open your web browser and visit http://www.tumblr.com.

**2** Enter your email address, a password and a URL for your Tumblr. For example, if you want to start a blog about hang gliding in Scotland, your Tumblr address might be scotlandHangGliding.Tumblr.com. If instead you want to blog about French fashion, try frenchFashion.Tumblr.com.

**3** If your Tumblr URL hasn't already been taken, you'll be approved within seconds. You should see a confirmation screen that prompts you to add your first blog post.

# Tip 10: Introduction to Google+

Google+ is the new social network created by Google. It features an interface that is similar to Facebook but that allows a much more intuitive way to create groups of friends (called Circles) with whom you can share photos, status updates, links and more.

At the time of writing, the only way to join Google+ is to be invited by someone already on the system, or to have a Google account.

If you have a Google account or have been invited, here's how to sign in:

**1** Point your browser at http://plus.google.com.

**2** Click Sign In.

**3** Enter your Google username and password.

# 1 Getting started with social media

| | |
|---|---|
| Who uses social media? | 15 |
| Why participate in social media? | 16 |
| Is social media 'viral'? | 17 |
| Privacy and security concerns | 18 |
| Finding your friends and colleagues on social media | 19 |
| Using social media to meet new friends | 21 |
| Using social media to follow a hobby or passion | 22 |
| Using social media to organise people for a cause or movement | 23 |
| Using social media to promote a business | 24 |

# Introduction

Unless you've been on a distant holiday without any access to the Internet or television news for the past five or so years, you've heard of social media. People have been talking incessantly, it seems, about Twitter, Facebook, YouTube and other services for years – they even made a fairly successful movie about Facebook called *The Social Network*. There are hundreds of millions of blogs, millions upon millions of shared videos on YouTube, and billions of photos posted and shared on Flickr and Instagram.

But what is social media, exactly? One way to define social media is any online tool that allows users to connect with each other and share information in a variety of formats. The emphasis in social media is on two-way communication – not only can you publish a blog story, but your readers can comment on that story and help disseminate what you've created with sharing tools.

- For example, on Twitter, you can share a link to something you find interesting. Others can reply to what you've said, starting a conversation about that link. Still others can retweet your original message and share with their followers.
- Similarly, on Facebook, you can upload a photo you took at your birthday party and then others can add their comments to that photo.

In this book, I'll be using the terms 'social media' and 'social networking' somewhat interchangeably, although in my mind (and in the minds of many others) the terms aren't quite equal. A social networking site (like Facebook or LinkedIn) emphasises connectivity between people and relationships, whereas a social media tool usually emphasises content creation and sharing (such as blogging or a video site). However, you really can't have relationships without creating content of some kind (even if it's just a short 140-character message) and content is meaningless if there's no one to share it with. So really the two aspects are intertwined.

**HOT TIP:** To learn more about social media, try googling some of the services you read about in this book. A quick Google search of Facebook or Twitter will bring up a ton of articles on those services, and especially how people use them in real life.

# Who uses social media?

Although the original users of social media were computer-literate people who were writing for a fairly small audience of those who were 'hip enough' to understand the world of blogs, that's not true any more.

The latest numbers give you some idea of how widespread social media is:

- Over 700 million Facebook users.
- Over 200 million Twitter users.
- Over 50 million LinkedIn users.
- Over 13 million hours of video were uploaded to YouTube in 2010.
- Flickr now hosts over 4 billion photos.

| City/Town | Facebook Users (inc. hometown & networks) |
|-----------|-------------------------------------------|
| Manchester | 2,067,000 |
| London | 1,894,000 |
| Birmingham | 1,151,440 |
| Sheffield | 673,000 |
| Edinburgh | 460,000 |
| Nottingham | 186,000 |
| Leeds | 184,000 |
| Liverpool | 151,000 |
| Bristol | 145,000 |
| Cardiff | 103,000 |

**? DID YOU KNOW?**

There are as many people on Facebook and Twitter as there are in the United States and the European Union combined.

# Why participate in social media?

People join social networks and consume/create social media content for a variety of reasons:

**1** They want to connect with old friends and family.

**2** They want to enhance their career networking prospects.

**3** They have something they want to share with the world – with social media they can blog about their interests (travel, love of gadgets, philosophy, etc.), share videos, share photos, and more.

**4** They want to meet other like-minded people and make new friends – this is usually based on shared interests or beliefs but the connection could also be geographic.

**5** They want to influence others with their opinions.

**6** They want to have an impact on their community.

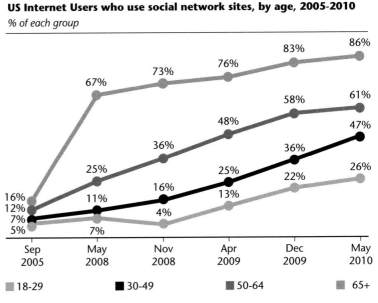

**US Internet Users who use social network sites, by age, 2005-2010**
*% of each group*

18-29: 16%, 67%, 73%, 76%, 83%, 86%
30-49: 12%, 25%, 36%, 48%, 58%, 61%
50-64: 7%, 11%, 16%, 25%, 36%, 47%
65+: 5%, 7%, 4%, 13%, 22%, 26%

Sep 2005 | May 2008 | Nov 2008 | Apr 2009 | Dec 2009 | May 2010

■ 18-29    ■ 30-49    ■ 50-64    ■ 65+

*Source: Pew Internet & American Life Proiject, "Older adults and socila media," Aug 27, 2010*

 **HOT TIP:** There's no rule that says you have to interact with everyone you meet on social media. Some will be old friends, others will be colleagues or recent friends, still others family, but it's likely you'll meet a lot of strangers. If someone doesn't make you feel comfortable, don't interact with them!

# Is social media 'viral'?

Some people confuse 'social media' with 'viral media' – the two don't have anything to do with each other. Occasionally, however, someone might post a video on YouTube (for example) that becomes an overnight sensation. When that happens, people talk about the video being a 'viral hit' or something along those lines, but the fact that it's on social media really has nothing to do with it going viral.

For most of you, don't worry about trying to create 'viral content' – it's best to be your most authentic self, sharing content that is important to you and to those in your social circle. That's the best way to gain a reputation as being a good person to know and follow and subscribe to.

However, if you want lots of retweets or Facebook/Google+ 'shares' then here's a quick way to do that:

1 Post something humorous. If it's an image, then even better.

2 Post something extremely useful, such as an article that helps people deal with a specific problem.

3 Post something unique. No one wants to see the 800th copy of that silly kitty picture. Find something original (or create something original) and share that.

4 It's even better if you can combine usefulness, humour and originality.

> **HOT TIP:** If you do a search for 'viral videos' on Google, you will see a whole list of videos that have 'gone viral' – a good way to waste an entire afternoon!

# Privacy and security concerns

Quite a few social media sites allow you to share quite a bit of information about yourself and what you're doing (and specifically, where you are doing it). For example, on Facebook, you can add all kinds of information to your profile (such as religious views, phone number, address, etc.) that you might not want to share with total strangers. Luckily, Facebook allows you some control over who can see this, but the settings are a bit confusing.

Other social media tools, especially location-based services like Gowalla and Foursquare, allow you to 'check in' to a restaurant, park, museum or other place you're visiting, and then share that check-in with your friends on Twitter and Facebook. Depending on how you share this information, checking in to locations using these tools can be an open invitation for others to know your movements, and that makes quite a few people uncomfortable.

Furthermore, other services may be adding location data to your content without your knowledge. If you take a photo with your smartphone and post it to Twitter, the image may contain geolocation information on where you took the photo. This is usually done out of convenience, but it could raise privacy issues if you took the photo at someone's house while you were visiting.

My advice?

1. Always review the privacy settings on each social network you join and make sure you understand how your information is being shared.

2. When you do share, ask yourself, 'does this photo/video/status update divulge too much information about me?' For example, do you really want the whole world to know that you are now on holiday and that your house is empty?

3. Keep in mind that passwords need to be updated on a regular basis to keep your accounts safe. And don't use easy-to-guess passwords like your mother's maiden name!

**! ALERT:** All social media sites have worked hard to institute some kind of privacy standard for their users, but someone has figured out workarounds for them all at one point or another.

# Finding your friends and colleagues on social media

Just about every single social media tool provides a mechanism for connecting with people.

For example, when you join Facebook:

**1** You can upload your email contacts and Facebook will try to find any users registered with those email addresses.

**2** You can use the Facebook search engine to find friends.

> **!** **ALERT:** Don't be surprised if some people refuse to connect with you on different social media sites. They may gladly follow you on Twitter or comment on your Tumblr blog, but they may allow only close friends and family members into their Facebook contacts.

3 You can browse your friends' friends list to see who you might know in common, and then send those people friend requests.

4 You might discover that a good friend of yours has a blog, and on that blog see a link to their Facebook profile.

Once you've connected with various people on Facebook, you can see who else those people have friended and then send mutual friends a connection request yourself.

Other social media tools (like Foursquare, Gowalla and Instagram, to name a few) allow you to search for friends who have connected with you on Facebook or Twitter. Simply provide these services with your Facebook and Twitter credentials and you'll find out which of your friends are using Gowalla (for example) and then connect with them there.

Why connect with the same people on different services? Simply put, different people use different social media tools to share different information. You may feel comfortable sharing only family-friendly content on Facebook, but use Twitter for content that aligns more with your political stance, and use Flickr to share your travel photography passion.

# Using social media to meet new friends

The hallmark of any good social media or social networking tool is the ability to connect with new people and make new friends. Most people use these techniques to enhance their networks:

**1** They use the built-in search tools for a service to discover new people. On Twitter, you may use the search tools to find people who are talking about a certain topic (travel writing, sports cars, a certain celebrity, etc.) and then start 'following' those people you find interesting. On Facebook, you might join different fan pages for companies you like and discover and interact with others who share your affinities and passions.

**2** They use the built-in 'suggested friends' feature for a social network. For example, on Facebook, you'll see a 'People You May Know' widget in the sidebar that lists people who are friends with your friends. Although you may not know any of these people, it's a good idea to look through the list to see if you've missed anyone.

**3** Whenever they meet people in real life, they find out how to connect with them on social networks. They might send someone a LinkedIn request, try to friend them on Facebook, or follow them on Twitter.

Of course, there are appropriate and inappropriate ways of doing this – depending on your social context or situation (you're a married man and you've just met a single young woman, for example), it may be untoward to ask for her Facebook details on the spot, particularly if she allows only close friends and family access to her information. On the other hand, she may also be on Twitter and feel comfortable giving you her Twitter handle so you can follow her there.

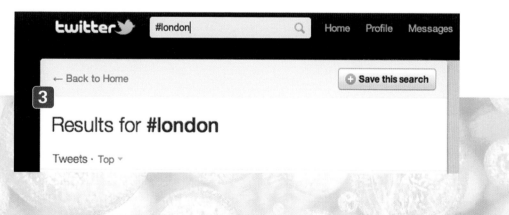

# Using social media to follow a hobby or passion

In much the same way you can find new friends on social media, you can also use most social media sites to keep up with your passions and hobbies.

**1** On Twitter, you can use the built-in search tools to search for keywords or hashtags being used by a certain community.

**2** On Facebook, you can search for your hobby and discover which community and fan pages have been set up and then join those discussions.

**3** You can also use Google or other search engines to perform searches that return blogs and other social content that match your interests.

 **HOT TIP:** Another good way to discover blogs and other sites devoted to a topic of interest is to use Google Alerts.

# Using social media to organise people for a cause or movement

Plenty of people are using social media tools like Twitter and Facebook to organise people for a cause or in support of a political candidate or movement.

For example:

- On Twitter, you'll often see petitions being sent around, and links asking for donations for this or that cause.
- On Facebook, many people have set up pages that extol the benefits of this or that politician or explain why supporting a certain non-profit organisation is good for the community.

Virtually any cause or movement can benefit from a social media-based effort. Don't think that your efforts have to be national or global in scope (although you'd be surprised to learn how many national and international efforts could use your help with something). Various successful efforts have been mounted to keep a dog park from being shut down in a local city, or in support of a candidate running for town council in a rural area.

**HOT TIP:** Before creating your own blog, Facebook page or other online meeting place, do some research to find out if someone has already set something up. If they have, join in and get to know the people involved. Later on, you might decide to start your own thing, but it's always good form to see what's already out there.

# Using social media to promote a business

Last but certainly not least, you can use social media to promote a business (either your own, or a business you love and frequent). Although there are some people who might object to the use of social media tools for this purpose, I don't think there's anything wrong with using your blog (for example) to explain your company's approach to XYZ.

Nor is it wrong to create a Twitter account or Facebook page where your customers can ask you questions, complain about lack of service or just simply connect with you and other customers on a more human level.

Furthermore, if you're a big fan of a company's products, there's nothing wrong with creating a blog (for example) that features blog posts, videos and other content of you using your favourite product. The company in question might react in different ways to your blog (for example, if they're open to social media they may support your efforts; if they're not, they may ask you to take it down) but for the most part, it's your blog. If someone objects to your focus on a company, then they can start their own blog with their own focus.

Just like with your personal social media, you'll need to follow some rules of 'social media physics':

**1** Different users like different services, and this holds true in the business world. If you just have a Facebook fan page, you won't get the attention of people who prefer Twitter or Google+. Diversify your social media portfolio.

**2** Stay away from non-business topics, such as religion, politics or other things that might cause lots of negative posts and comments. If you run a bakery, then tell us about your business, tell us about new products and offers, and tell us how to enjoy baked goods. Even posting articles about the history of bakeries in your local region is fair game.

**3** Monitor what's happening. You will get trolls and spammers who try to fill your blog or Facebook fan page with garbage posts. You will also get real customers on there asking you legitimate questions, and you don't want to keep them hanging. Keep up with what's happening.

# 2 Twitter

Set up a Twitter account                   29

Tweet!                                     30

Tweet a reply to a specific person         31

Use a Twitter hashtag                      32

Finding friends on Twitter                 33

Using Twitter search                       36

Sending a direct message                   37

Installing Tweetdeck                       38

Using Twitter on an iPhone                 40

# Introduction

Twitter is located on the web at Twitter.com. Technically it's a social networking and microblogging service.

Although 140 characters doesn't seem like much, in no time you'll get the hang of it. What do people post on Twitter?

1. Status updates of what they're doing right now ('having lunch with an old friend').

2. Plain old thoughts about how they're feeling or what kind of day they've had.

3. Links to interesting content on news sites, blogs or videos.

4. Photos that they've taken with their smartphones.

5. Replies to other Twitter users.

6. Retweets of tweets by other users.

7. Messages from other social media services, such as what song they are listening to on Blip.fm, where they've checked in using Gowalla, and so on.

**? DID YOU KNOW?**

Microblogging is, as its name implies, just like blogging, except you don't need to create fully fledged blog content in order to use it. In fact, all you have to do on Twitter is post messages that are 140 characters or less.

**? DID YOU KNOW?**

At the time I'm writing this, Twitter users generate 200 million tweets per day.

# Set up a Twitter account

Twitter is one of the fastest-growing services in the social media universe. Setting up an account is very easy. All you have to do is:

**1** Open a web browser and visit http://twitter.com.

**2** Under the headline New to Twitter? you'll find a form.

**3** Fill out your name, email address and a password and click Sign up.

Once you've signed up, start following people who are of interest to you. Twitter will show you a list of featured Twitter users as part of the sign-up process. Don't forget to add a bio and upload an avatar.

If you like, go ahead and follow @myerman (that's me) and say hello!

**ALERT:** You must use a unique email address to get an account on Twitter.

**ALERT:** When someone follows you on Twitter, there's no obligation for you to follow them back. So don't be thrown off if someone doesn't follow you back. It's always a good idea to say hello so they know who you are.

# Tweet!

Now that you're on Twitter, it's time to send out a tweet. A tweet is a Twitter message. Please don't say 'twit' or that you 'twit'. Your message has to be 140 characters or less.

To send out a tweet:

**1** Make sure you're logged into Twitter.

**2** Under What's happening? you'll notice a blank text field. Click that field.

**3** Compose your message, keeping it to 140 characters or less. Most people tell others what they're doing at the moment (reading a book, enjoying the outdoors or going shopping) or share a link or photo.

**4** Once you're happy with your tweet, click the Tweet button.

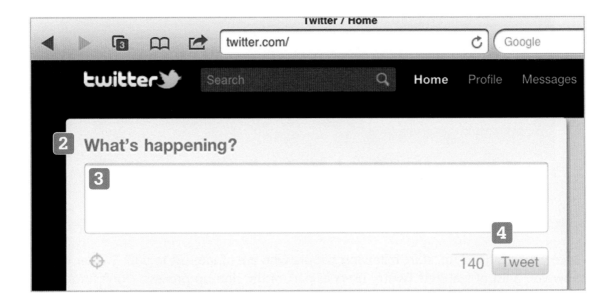

**? DID YOU KNOW?**

The 140-character limit comes from the old SMS/text-messaging days of Twitter.

# Tweet a reply to a specific person

Sometimes you don't want to send a message to everyone who is following you, but instead want to send a tweet for someone's attention. You can do this by starting your tweet with the person's @ name (in other words, their twitter handle – mine is @ myerman).

To send a reply:

**1** Make sure you're logged into Twitter.

**2** You'll notice a blank text field. Click that field.

**3** Compose your message, keeping it to 140 characters or less. Usually people start a reply with the recipient's @ name, but this isn't necessary.

**4** Once you're happy with your tweet, click the Tweet button.

**ALERT:** Sending someone an @ reply is still public and anyone can read it, but putting their @ name in the tweet will increase the likelihood that they will see it, especially if they have a busy timeline.

# Use a Twitter hashtag

Twitter hashtags were invented to help busy Twitter users organise their conversations. In the Twitter world, it's very easy to follow lots of different people with lots of different interests. Although you can use the search functions on Twitter to find out what's interesting to you (for example, you might do a search for 'kayaks' or 'gardening' or 'travel'), different groups will probably have adopted special hashtags for different hobbies, events or topics.

For example, an author who is touring the country and giving lectures might create her own hashtag (#booktour2011, for instance), using that hashtag in her tweets. Her fans might also tweet using that hashtag. By searching for that hashtag, you not only get to see what the author is doing, but also meet and interact with a whole bunch of people you might never otherwise have met.

To use a hashtag in your tweets:

1 Make sure you're logged into Twitter.

2 Under What's happening? you'll notice a blank text field. Click that field.

3 Compose your message, keeping it to 140 characters or less. Add your hashtag to the tweet wherever you like. Many people put them at the end, but that isn't necessary.

4 Once you're happy with your tweet, click the Tweet button.

**? DID YOU KNOW?**

There isn't an official registry of hashtags. You'll learn which ones your specific community of users has adopted.

# Finding friends on Twitter

The easiest way to find new friends on Twitter:

**1** Make sure you're logged into Twitter.

**2** Click the Find New Friends button on the web interface.

**3** Click the Find Friends tab.

**4** Use one of the search tools to look for friends who have already signed up using an email address. You can currently use Gmail, Yahoo, Hotmail, AOL or LinkedIn to find friends.

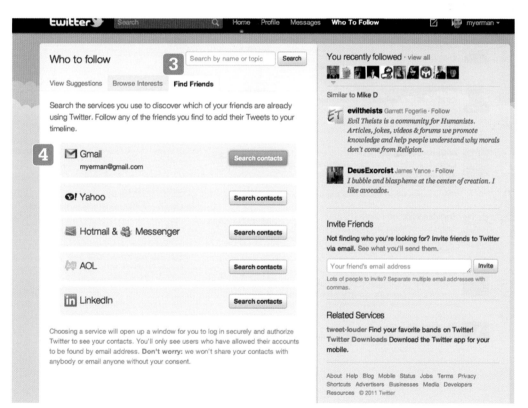

**? DID YOU KNOW?**

Another effective way to make friends on Twitter is to attend a tweetup. They're organised all the time in cities across the world. Attending a tweetup is lots of fun because then you can finally put names and faces to Twitter handles.

**5** You can also click the View Suggestions tab to see who else might interest you based on who you already follow. For example, if you already follow various science fiction authors, you'll probably end up with a few other authors in the suggestions list.

**6** You can also click the Browse Interests tab and browse through various categories of Twitter users based on topics. For example, Art & Design, Books, Business, Charity, and more.

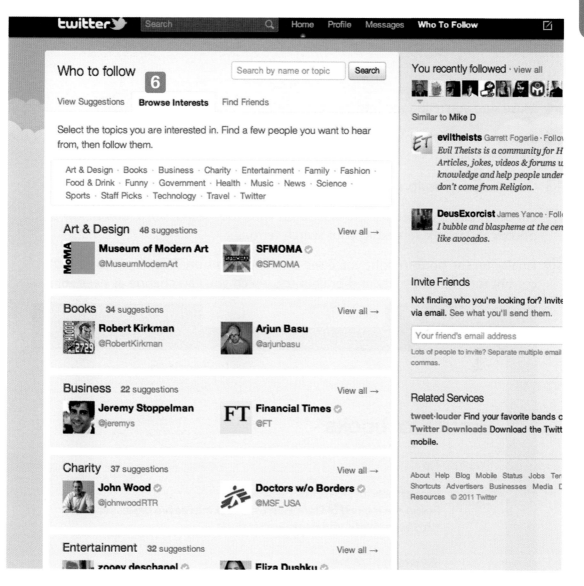

# Using Twitter search

Once you're logged into Twitter, you can use its powerful search features to help you find tweets (and the people who own those accounts) that match the search term you are interested in.

To search on Twitter:

**1** Make sure you're logged into Twitter.

**2** Type a search term into the search field next to the Twitter logo along the top of the web page.

**3** On the search results page, you'll see tweets listed on the left.

**4** On the right, you'll see people associated with your search term, and below that, photos and videos related to your search term.

**5** Finally, on the bottom right you'll see trending terms on Twitter – these are the current top tweets by city and/or country, which you can change as needed.

**? DID YOU KNOW?**

The search interface will continuously update. You can click the refresh now button to refresh the search listing.

# Sending a direct message

Sending someone a reply is useful, but the information you're sending them is still public. Anyone who is following both you and the person you've sent the reply to will see what you're talking about. Sometimes this is appropriate, but in other cases you probably want more privacy.

Luckily, Twitter allows you to send direct messages (DMs for short) that are private between you and the person you're communicating with.

To send a direct message:

**1** Make sure you're logged into Twitter.

**2** Start a new message with a d followed by a space followed by the person's twitter handle minus the @ symbol. So if you want to send me (@myerman) a DM, you'd start your tweet with: d myerman

**3** Follow this up with your message. Make sure the entire message is 140 characters or less.

**ALERT:** You can only send DMs to people who are following you!

# Installing Tweetdeck

There's no rule that says you have to use Twitter directly on Twitter.com. In fact, many people use a 'Twitter client' on their desktop or laptop to access Twitter. By using one of these, you can organise your tweets, save searches and do a whole lot more besides. One of the most popular Twitter clients is Tweetdeck.

To install Tweetdeck:

**1** Open up your browser and go to http://www.tweetdeck.com.

**2** In the navigation pane along the top, click on Desktop.

**3** Click Download now.

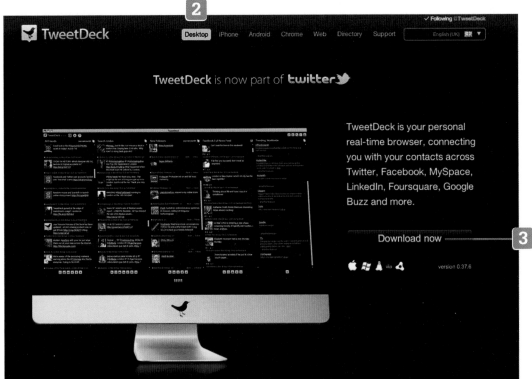

**4** Once you've installed Tweetdeck, you will need to add your Twitter credentials (username and password you registered with Twitter).

**5** As soon as you do that, Tweetdeck will connect with Twitter and start pulling down different tweets into different columns:

- your main timeline (tweets from everyone you follow)
- mentions (every tweet that mentions your Twitter handle)
- direct messages to you
- you can also create special columns that contains a search term, Twitter group, or other sets of tweets.

# Using Twitter on an iPhone

One of the best things about being on Twitter is how small and compact each message is – it's tailor-made for a mobile device. That's not surprising given its origins as an SMS-based messaging system.

You can of course simply use your iPhone (or Android, for that matter) to go to http:// twitter.com, but to get the most out of your Twitter experience, it's a good idea to download a Twitter application.

The most popular Twitter application is Twitter, and it's free. Simply download it from the App Store on your phone, log in with your Twitter username and password, and you'll be ready to use Twitter on your phone.

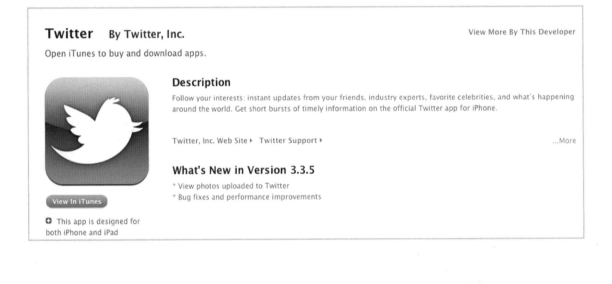

**Twitter**   **By Twitter, Inc.**                      View More By This Developer

Open iTunes to buy and download apps.

### Description

Follow your interests: instant updates from your friends, industry experts, favorite celebrities, and what's happening around the world. Get short bursts of timely information on the official Twitter app for iPhone.

Twitter, Inc. Web Site ▸   Twitter Support ▸                           ...More

### What's New in Version 3.3.5

* View photos uploaded to Twitter
* Bug fixes and performance improvements

➕ This app is designed for both iPhone and iPad

**? DID YOU KNOW?**

The current Twitter application used to be called Tweetie, but Twitter acquired that company too!

# 3 Facebook basics

| | |
|---|---|
| Set up a Facebook account | 43 |
| Adding a bio | 44 |
| Uploading a profile picture | 45 |
| Finding friends on Facebook | 46 |
| Share what you're doing on Facebook | 47 |
| Adding a comment to a friend's Facebook status | 48 |
| Viewing a friend's profile | 49 |
| Friending someone on Facebook | 50 |
| Liking on Facebook | 51 |
| Share photos on Facebook | 52 |
| Share videos on Facebook | 53 |
| Share links on Facebook | 54 |
| Tagging people on Facebook | 55 |

# Introduction

If you've seen the film *The Social Network* then you know the rough outlines of the story of Facebook: Mark Zuckerberg, an undergraduate at Harvard University, created Facebook along with a few of his friends in order to provide a place where people could connect with their college friends after they'd left university. The term 'facebook' came from a kind of university yearbook.

Facebook was originally meant only for university students, and remained exclusively so for the first few years of its existence. In 2006 Facebook became open to anyone over the age of 13 with a valid email address.

At the time of writing, over 700 million users worldwide are members of Facebook. The site has an estimated 138 million monthly unique site visitors in the United States alone.

**? DID YOU KNOW?**
The original name of Facebook was TheFacebook.

# Set up a Facebook account

Facebook is the most popular social networking site in the world, with 600 million users (and counting) worldwide. You're more likely to run into old school friends, relatives and colleagues on Facebook than on just about any other place.

To set up a Facebook account:

**1** Open a web browser and visit http://www.facebook.com.

**2** Enter your first and last name in the Sign Up form.

**3** Enter your email address, then confirm it.

**4** Enter a password.

**5** Select your gender from the drop-down list.

**6** Enter your birthday (it's used to verify that you are over 18).

**7** Click Sign Up.

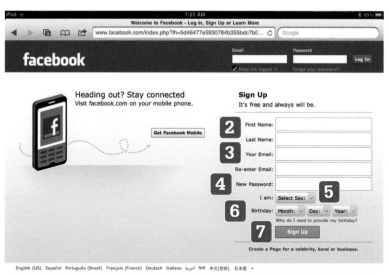

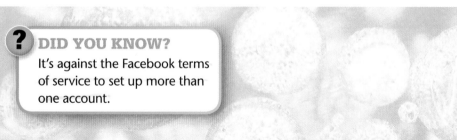

**? DID YOU KNOW?**
It's against the Facebook terms of service to set up more than one account.

# Adding a bio

Once you've set up your account, it's time to add some information about yourself.

To edit your profile:

**1** Make sure you're logged on to Facebook.

**2** In the upper right corner, click your name.

**3** Click Edit Profile.

**4** Enter as much or as little information as you want about your current city, home town, gender, birthday, languages you speak. Don't forget to add a short bio, 2–3 sentences long.

Thomas Myer ▶ **Edit Profile**                                    ◀ **View My Profile**

- Basic Information
- Profile Picture
- Friends and Family
- Education and Work
- Philosophy
- Arts and Entertainment
- Sports
- Activities and Interests
- Contact Information

Visit your privacy settings to control who can see the information on your profile.

Current City: Austin, Texas ✕    **4**

Hometown: Las Tablas, Los Santos, Panama ✕

I Am: Male ⬍                    ☑ Show my sex in my profile

Birthday: Jun ⬍ 5 ⬍ 1971 ⬍

Show my full birthday in my profile. ⬍

Interested In: ☐ Women
☐ Men

Languages:
American English ✕
Spanish ✕
British English ✕
JRR Tolkien/Quenya ✕
In Star Wars ✕
Klingon ✕
Vulgar Latin ✕

About Me: Curmudgeon. Stick in the mud. Scoundrel. Introvert. Fugitive from

**? DID YOU KNOW?**

You can have a lot of fun with the languages – you can even include made-up languages from *Star Wars*, *Star Trek* and Tolkien. Impress your friends with your Klingon fluency!

# Uploading a profile picture

Your Facebook profile isn't complete until you've uploaded a photo of yourself.

To upload a photo:

**1** Make sure you're logged on to Facebook.

**2** In the upper right corner, click the Profile link.

**3** Click Edit Profile.

**4** On the far left, click Profile Picture.

**5** Click Choose File and then browse for a photo on your computer OR click Take a Picture (you can only use this option if your computer has a built-in camera).

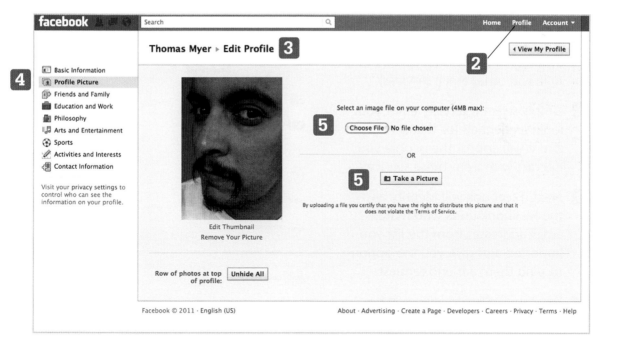

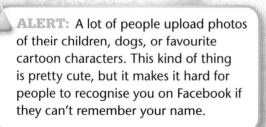

**ALERT:** A lot of people upload photos of their children, dogs, or favourite cartoon characters. This kind of thing is pretty cute, but it makes it hard for people to recognise you on Facebook if they can't remember your name.

# Finding friends on Facebook

Being on Facebook is no fun unless you can interact with friends. So how do you find people you already know on Facebook? It's easy, once you know how to use the Find Friends feature.

To find friends on Facebook:

**1** Make sure you're logged on to Facebook.

**2** Be sure you click your name in the upper right-hand corner, then click Friends in the left navigation pane.

**3** The words Find Friends will show up underneath. Go ahead and click that.

**4** You can now import contacts from a variety of services (Skype, Yahoo, AOL and other email services).

**5** Simply select a service, enter your login credentials for that service, and it will import the people you interact with from those services.

**6** Next, Facebook will identify all the Facebook users who match email addresses from the list you imported and give you the option to send them a friend request.

**7** You can also invite anyone who doesn't have a matching email address to become a member of Facebook.

**? DID YOU KNOW?**

Facebook doesn't save your login credentials for these services.

# Share what you're doing on Facebook

Now that you're on Facebook, it's time to tell your friends and family what it is you're up to. Facebook lets you do that with its Share button.

To update your status:

**1** Make sure you're logged on to Facebook.

**2** You'll notice that at the top of the page is a series of options. Click Update Status.

**3** In the Status field is some placeholder text: What's on your mind? Simply click in the status field and replace that text with your own, for example: 'Going to the market today, with any luck I can find some fresh seasonal vegetables there!'

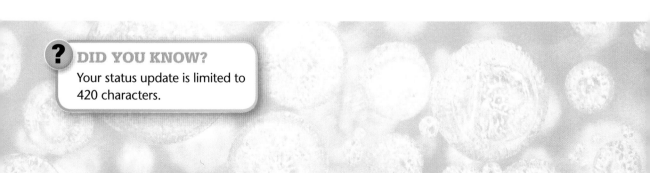

**? DID YOU KNOW?**
Your status update is limited to 420 characters.

# Adding a comment to a friend's Facebook status

Posting a status update is part of being on Facebook, but so is adding comments to someone else's Facebook status. Comments allow you and all your friends to have a conversation about the original status update, link, photo or video.

To add a comment:

**1** Make sure you're logged on to Facebook.

**2** Find a status update posted by one of your friends.

**3** Underneath the post you'll see a blank text field with the prompt 'Write a comment …' in it.

**4** Click in the text field and write your comment.

**5** Press the Enter key to add the comment.

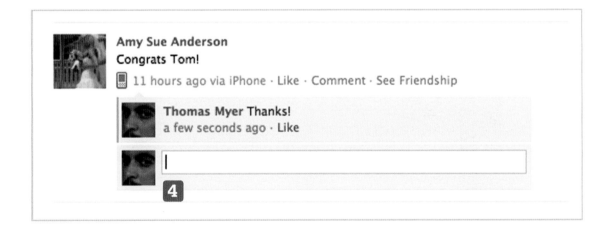

**Amy Sue Anderson**
**Congrats Tom!**
11 hours ago via iPhone · Like · Comment · See Friendship

**Thomas Myer Thanks!**
a few seconds ago · Like

**? DID YOU KNOW?**
You can delete a comment by clicking the X on the right edge of the comment. Just hover over your comment and the X will appear.

**! ALERT:** Facebook comments are non-hierarchical. In other words, you can't directly respond to someone else's comment like you can on some blogs. Instead, all the comments form a stream.

# Viewing a friend's profile

Sometimes you want to learn more about the people you are friends with on Facebook. They may be people you know in real life, or have over for dinner all the time, but do you really know everything about them? Like their favourite music, TV shows and books?

Luckily, Facebook allows you to view your friends' profiles. To view a profile:

**1** Make sure you're logged on to Facebook.

**2** Click a friend's name or avatar on Facebook.

**3** At the top of their profile you'll see a summary of where they work, what school they went to, where they live currently, their marital status, their languages, home town and birthday.

**4** If you want to know more, click Info in the left navigation pane.

**5** You can scroll down to see their schools; religious and political views; sports they play; favourite music, books and movies; favourite activities and interests; and their bio and contact information.

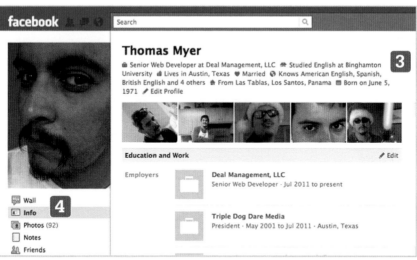

# Friending someone on Facebook

Occasionally you'll run into someone you know in real life and will want to 'friend' them on Facebook. You can't become someone's friend until they approve your request, so you have to send in the request and then wait for them to approve you.

To friend someone on Facebook:

**1** Make sure you're logged on to Facebook.

**2** Click a person's name or avatar.

**3** Click Add Friend on their profile.

**4** Click Send Request.

**5** You'll see a note that says your friend request has been sent.

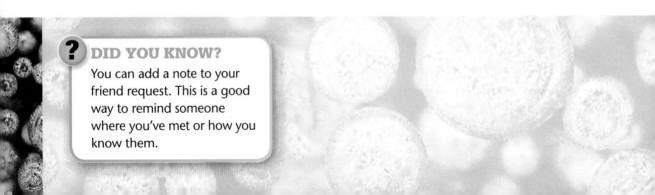

**DID YOU KNOW?**

You can add a note to your friend request. This is a good way to remind someone where you've met or how you know them.

# Liking on Facebook

You're not just limited to commenting on someone's status updates – you can also 'like' what people have posted. A like works like a vote in favour of something. For example, your friend might post that they've just been promoted, or got a new puppy – either of these would warrant a like. Also note that you can like someone's comment – maybe they've said something clever in response to one of your posts.

To like something on Facebook:

**1** Make sure you're logged on to Facebook.

**2** Find a status update or comment that you think merits a like.

**3** Click the Like link for that item.

**4** Once you like something, Facebook will tell you that 'You like this'. If others have liked the item, you'll see their names listed too.

**? DID YOU KNOW?**
Once you've liked something, you can unlike it. However, you can't cast a 'negative vote' (an unlike) to begin with.

**? DID YOU KNOW?**
A Facebook like is an easy way to interact with friends when you don't have time to actually leave a comment.

# Share photos on Facebook

Once you're on Facebook, you can share all kinds of interesting news and items with your friends and family. One thing people share a lot of is photos.

To share a photo:

**1** Make sure you're logged on to Facebook.

**2** At the very top of the page you'll see Add Photo/Video – click that link.

**3** You then have the option of uploading a photo, taking a photo with your webcam or creating an album with many photos in it. For now, let's upload a photo.

**4** Click Upload a Photo. Click Choose File and then browse through your computer's folders to find the image you want to upload.

**5** You can also add a caption to the photo.

**6** Click Share when you're ready to share this photo with friends.

**2**

📝 Update Status   📷 Add Photo / Video   📊 Ask Question

| Upload Photo / Video | Use Webcam | Create Photo Album |

**4**

**!** **ALERT:** You've probably read stories in the news about people getting into trouble for the pictures they post on Facebook. Just assume that every photo you post on Facebook can be shared with anyone else.

# Share videos on Facebook

More and more of us have easy access to digital video recorders and smartphones with video-recording capabilities. The process of shooting a short video and then sharing it with all your friends on Facebook couldn't be easier:

**1** Make sure you're logged on to Facebook.

**2** At the very top of the page you'll see Add Photo/Video. Click that link.

**3** You can record a video with your webcam, or upload a video. For now, let's just upload a video.

**4** Click Upload Photo/Video.

**5** Click Choose File and then browse your hard drive for the video you want to upload.

**6** Add a caption to the video and click Post.

**2**

Update Status | Add Photo / Video | Ask Question

Say something about this...

Select an image or video file on your computer.

Choose File | no file selected **5**

**6**

👤+ 📍 Austin | 👥 Friends ▼ | Post

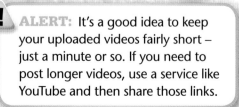

**ALERT:** It's a good idea to keep your uploaded videos fairly short – just a minute or so. If you need to post longer videos, use a service like YouTube and then share those links.

# Share links on Facebook

Just read something on the Web (a blog post, perhaps, or a news story?) and want to share that link with your Facebook friends? That's easy with Facebook link sharing:

**1** Make sure you're logged on to Facebook.

**2** At the very top of the page you'll see an Update Status link. Click that link.

**3** Enter (or copy and paste) the URL you wish to share.

**4** Add some text and click Post.

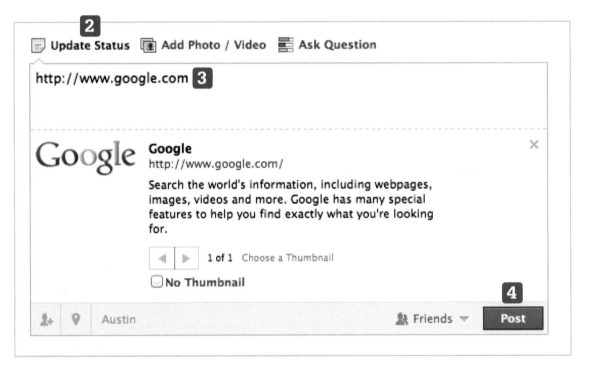

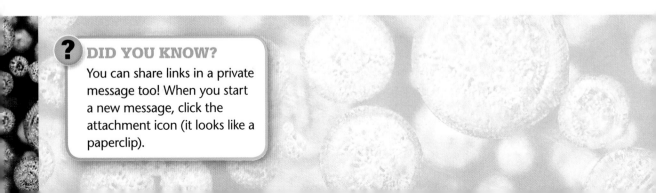

**? DID YOU KNOW?**

You can share links in a private message too! When you start a new message, click the attachment icon (it looks like a paperclip).

# Tagging people on Facebook

When you upload an image or video, Facebook allows you to 'tag' the people who are in that photo or video. For example, you may post a picture of you and two of your friends having happy-hour cocktails. You want to make sure your friends see that you've uploaded this image – this is where Facebook tagging comes into play.

To tag people on Facebook:

1. Make sure you're logged on to Facebook.

2. Select an image you've uploaded to Facebook by clicking on Photos and then browsing through your galleries.

3. Click Tag this Photo.

4. Click a person's face in the photo.

5. Type that person's name into the 'provide text' field. As you type, Facebook will narrow down your list of friends.

6. Once you've finished, click Done Tagging.

ALERT: Some people on Facebook object to being tagged in photos. Don't be surprised if they untag themselves by visiting your photo and clicking Remove Tag next to their name on a photo.

# 4 Advanced Facebook

Using the notes feature to 'blog' on Facebook      59

Asking a question on Facebook      61

Posting to someone's wall      62

Tagging someone in a post or a comment      63

Sending a private message      64

Creating an event on Facebook      66

Liking a fan page      68

Telling others about a fan page      69

Facebook on your iPhone      70

# Introduction

Now that you know more about the basis of Facebook, in this chapter you'll learn about more advanced features, such as notes, working with Facebook on your mobile device, fan pages, private messages, and more.

# Using the notes feature to 'blog' on Facebook

You may or may not have a blog already. Maybe you don't really know what a blog is all about, but did you know that Facebook gives you the chance to create a blog of sorts? By using the Notes feature, you can create longer entries than are allowed with Status Updates.

Notes allow you to share stories, poems, or diary entries from your journal. Your friends can share your notes, comment on them and like them, just like anything else on Facebook.

To create a note:

**Thomas Myer ▸ Notes**

**How not to Recruit Talent**
By Thomas Myer· Thursday, June 9, 2011

There's a company in town, [NAME REDACTED] who has been wooing me. I keep being aloof as I'm not interested in a full-time gig. So finally the recruiter breaks me down and I'm having lunch today when she calls and says we are on for an interview tomorrow. She'll send me an important email from the company ASAP, and that I MUST READ IT BEFORE I SHOW...

View Full Note · 🔒 · Like · Comment

👍 Amy Gelfand, Claire England, Noah Masterson and 2 others like this.

💬 View all 55 comments

Write a comment...

**Getting to Know You/Me/Whatever**
By Thomas Myer· Friday, August 21, 2009

If you've been tagged or you are reading this, you have the honor of copying all these goofy questions, writing your own response, and tagging 10 other victims. You have to tag me. If I tagged you, it's because I want to know more about you – in a creepy stalker kind of way.
To do this, go to "notes" under tabs on your profile page, paste these inst...

View Full Note · 🔒 · Like · Comment

💬 View all 2 comments

Write a comment...

1 Make sure you're logged on to Facebook.

2 Click your name in the upper right corner.

3 Click Notes in the left navigation pane.

4 Click Write a Note.

5 Enter a title.

6 Write your note in the body. You're allowed to use minimal HTML markup (bolding, italicising, underlining, creating bullet lists and so on).

7  Add any tags that would describe your note. A tag is like a keyword. So if your note is about your new job, you might tag it with career, new job and jobs.

8  Add a photo to your post if you like.

9  Set your privacy for the note – who can see the note?

10  If you're ready to publish the note, click Publish. You can also Preview the piece and make changes or save the note as a draft.

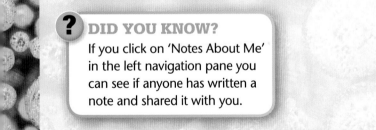

# Asking a question on Facebook

Facebook's new question feature is a quick way to learn from your friends. Think of it as being able to harness the power of your Facebook network to run little mini-polls. These polls can be as silly as 'what is your favourite flavour of ice cream?' or as serious as what your friends' preferences are in the next election.

To ask a question:

**1** Make sure you're logged on to Facebook.

**2** At the top of the page you'll see Ask Question. Click that link.

**3** If you want to ask an open-ended question, enter your question in the text field and click Post.

**4** If you want to provide multiple-choice options for your friends to answer, click Add Poll Options and then add a few options.

---

**2**

📝 Update Status   📷 Add Photo / Video   ☰ **Ask Question**

| What is your favorite flavor of ice cream? **3** |
| --- |
| Vanilla |
| **4** Chocolate |
| Butter Pecan| |
| Add an option... |
| Add an option... |
| ☑ Allow anyone to add options          👥 Friends ▼   **Post** |

# Posting to someone's wall

Sometimes you want to post information not to your stream, but to someone's wall. You can easily do this by switching to their wall and then posting a status update, photo, video or link there.

To post an item to someone's wall:

**1** Make sure you're logged on to Facebook.

**2** Click a person's name or avatar.

**3** Now you're on their wall. At the top you'll see some sharing options.

**4** Choose the option that is right for you – post, photo or video.

**5** Follow the same procedure that you'd use to post something to your own stream.

**ALERT:** When you post to someone's wall, everyone who is a friend of theirs will see it – it is not a private message.

# Tagging someone in a post or a comment

Sometimes you want to post an item (such as a video or photo) to your own stream but you want to make sure that certain friends see what you've posted. Facebook now allows you to tag someone in a post or comment, like you might in a photograph.

To tag a friend in a post or comment:

**1** Make sure you're logged on to Facebook.

**2** Share a post, link, video or photo as you normally would.

**3** Before you post your information, make sure that you tag someone using the @ symbol. When you press that key, Facebook will provide you with a pop-up menu of friends who match your search criteria.

**4** When you've found the friend you want to tag, click their name in the list. Facebook will add their name to the update as a link.

**5** When you publish the post, Facebook will notify them that they've been tagged by you.

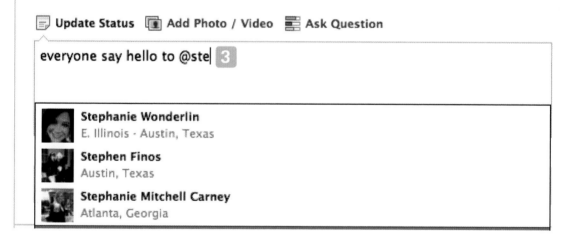

**ALERT:** When you tag someone in a post or comment, they get an alert every time someone else likes or comments, which might be a bit annoying for them.

# Sending a private message

Posting stuff to your own or a friend's wall is sufficient for most cases, but sometimes you want to send a private message to someone (or to a group of people). This is especially true if you want to share private information (such as your phone number) or maybe share a link or other information that isn't appropriate for a wider audience.

To send a private message on Facebook:

1 Make sure you're logged on to Facebook.

2 Click the Messages icon in the upper left, close to the Facebook logo.

3 In the pop-up box, click Send a New Message.

**? DID YOU KNOW?**

You can include several people in a private message. They have the option of leaving a conversation, too.

4 A new pop-up box will appear. Type the recipient's name in the To field (Facebook will automatically fill in your friend's name as you type).

5 Add a message.

6 Attach a document, photograph or link if you need to.

7 Click the Send button when you're ready to send it.

# Creating an event on Facebook

There are lots of important events in your life (birthdays, anniversaries) and not-so-important but equally fun events (guys' poker night, happy-hour get-togethers) and Facebook can help you organise those occasions with its events features.

To create an event on Facebook:

**1** Make sure you're logged on to Facebook.

**2** In the left navigation pane, click on Events.

**3** Click Create an Event.

**4** Set a date and time for your event.

**5** Give your event a title.

**6** Tell people where the event will be (you can even add a specific street address).

**Create an Event**

**31**

+ Add Event Photo

**4** When?  7/9/2011   1:00 am ⬍  Add end time

**5** What are you planning?

Where? **6**

Add street address

More info?

Who's invited?   Select Guests

☑ Anyone can view and RSVP (public event)
☑ Show the guest list on the event page

Create Event

Facebook © 2011 · English (US)        About · Advertising · Create a Page · Developers · Careers · Privacy · Terms · Help

**? DID YOU KNOW?**

Everyone who is invited to the event gets a Facebook message letting them know they need to RSVP.

7 Add more specific information (like what people should bring, or directions to help those who might get lost).

8 Click Select Guests to choose which friends are invited to your event.

9 If this is a private event, untick the box next to Anyone can view and RSVP.

10 Add an event photo by clicking Add Event Photo.

11 When you're ready to publish your event, click Create Event.

**Create an Event**

| | |
|---|---|
| **31** | When? 7/9/2011 📅 1:00 am ⇕ Add end time |
| 10 + Add Event Photo | What are you planning? |
| | Where? |
| | Add street address |
| 7 More info? | |
| | Who's invited? 8 Select Guests |
| | ☑ Anyone can view and RSVP (public event) |
| | ☑ Show the guest list on the event page 9 |
| | Create Event 11 |

Facebook © 2011 · English (US)

About · Advertising · Create a Page · Developers · Careers · Privacy · Terms · Help

# Liking a fan page

Businesses can create 'fan pages' on Facebook. Think of them as profile pages for a business or a brand. For example, a major brand like Coca-Cola or Nike will probably have a fan page, but so might your local flower shop, bank or town newspaper.

To find a fan page, do a search for your favourite brands (for example, you might be a photographer who uses Nikon cameras, or a runner who only wears Under Armour running shorts) and see if they have a fan page.

**DID YOU KNOW?**

You can usually leave a comment or interact with that fan page once you've clicked the Like button on that page.

# Telling others about a fan page

Once you 'like' a fan page, it'll probably show up in your stream that you've liked it, which means that others will see it. However, you can do more than that – you can share a fan page with someone else. For example, a few weeks ago, I discovered that my favourite manufacturer of affordable kilts (Stillwater Kilts) was on Facebook. I decided to share that knowledge with a few of my friends who also like to wear kilts.

To tell others about a fan page:

1 Make sure you're logged on to Facebook.

2 Navigate to the page you want to tell others about.

3 In the left navigation pane for the page, click Share.

4 A pop-up window will appear. You can now add a note and then share the page on your wall, a friend's wall, or in a private message to one or more people.

**Share this Page**

3 Share: **On your own Wall** ▼ 🔒 ▼

4 Write Something...

# Facebook on your iPhone

You can download Facebook for your iPhone and take your friends wherever you go – most if not all of the most important features of Facebook (sharing posts, uploading video and photos, sending private messages, and lots more besides) are available directly via the app.

To download Facebook:

1. On your iPhone, visit the App Store.

2. Do a search for Facebook. It's a free application.

3. Download the application to your iPhone.

4. Once you've downloaded it, tap it to start and then enter your Facebook credentials.

**Description**

Facebook for iPhone makes it easy to stay connected and share information with friends. Use your iPhone to start a conversation with Facebook Chat, check your friends' latest photos and status updates, look up a phone number, or upload your own mobile photos to Facebook while on the go.

Facebook, Inc. Web Site ▸  Facebook Support ▸

**What's New in Version 3.4.3**

- Various bug fixes
- Improved security

View In iTunes

**Free**
Category: Social Networking
Updated: Jun 29, 2011
Current Version: 3.4.3
3.4.3
Size: 6.3 MB
Languages: English, Chinese, Dutch, French, German, Italian, Japanese, Korean, Polish, Portuguese, Russian, Spanish, Turkish
Seller: Facebook, Inc.
© Facebook, Inc.
Rated 4+

**Requirements:** Compatible with iPhone, iPod touch, and iPad. Requires iOS 3.0 or later

**Customer Ratings**

Current Version:
★★ 14956 Ratings
All Versions:
★★★★ 1763836 Ratings

**iPhone Screenshots**

Account   **facebook**   +

Q Search

News Feed    Profile    Friends

Messages    Places    Groups

31

**facebook**   Live Fe

Photo    Status    Check I

**Paul Carduner**
San Francisco, CA
Paul checked in at San Francisco, CA.
👤 3 hours ago
💬 1 comment

**Gabriel Trionfi Hitting**
Piedmont for some Halloween fun with Hillary and Paul. After a great brunch.

? **DID YOU KNOW?**

You can use most Facebook functions right from your iPhone. In fact, many people simply use a mobile app to experience Facebook.

# 5 Google+

Getting to know Google+                                      73

Sharing on Google+                                           74

Sharing a photo on Google+                                   75

Sharing a photo album on Google+                             76

Viewing photos from your circle on Google+                   77

Sharing a video on Google+                                   78

Adding comments on Google+                                   79

Adding a +1 on Google+                                       80

Muting a post on Google+                                     81

Sharing on Google+                                           82

Restrict sharing on Google+                                  83

Working with circles in Google+                              84

Notifications in Google+                                     86

Viewing a specific stream on Google+                         87

Viewing your own profile on Google+                          88

Starting a hangout on Google+                                89

Sparks on Google+                                            90

Your Google+ settings                                        92

# Introduction

Google+ is the new social network created by Google. It features an interface that is similar to Facebook but that allows a much more intuitive way to create groups of friends (called circles) with whom you can share photos, status updates, links and more.

At the time of writing, the only way to join Google+ is to be invited by someone already on the system, or to have a Google account.

If you have a Google account or have been invited, here's how to sign in:

**1** Point your browser at http://plus.google.com.

**2** Click Sign In.

**3** Enter your Google username and password.

# Getting to know Google+

Once you're logged in, you'll see the Google+ home page. It consists of the following sections:

- A top navigation bar. You can switch between the home view, photos, profile and circles. You can also run a search.
- On the left are streams from your circles, sparks (these are special interest searches) and chat.
- The centre portion of the interface allows you to share information with your circles. Below that is a stream from everyone you have included in a circle.
- On the right you can see a summary of people in your circles and hangouts.

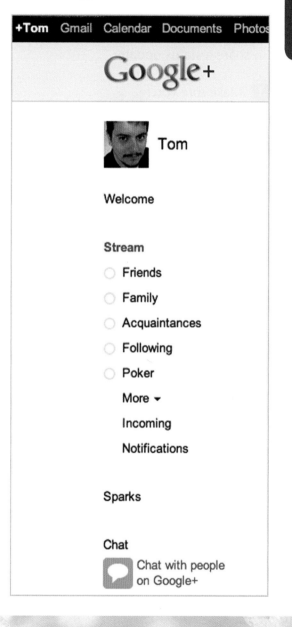

---

**WHAT DOES THIS MEAN?**

**Circle:** A group of friends. For example, you may put various people in a circle called 'co-workers' and put another group of people in 'close friends'. People can belong to multiple circles. When you post status updates on Google+ you can send information to specific circles.

# Sharing on Google+

Sharing information on Google+ is very much like sharing on Facebook.

To share a status update:

**1** Make sure you're logged on to Google+.

**2** Click the box that contains the words 'Share what's new ...'.

**3** Enter a status update.

**4** Choose which circles to share with.

**5** Click Share.

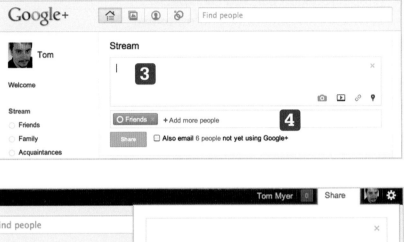

# Sharing a photo on Google+

If you're anything like me, you take a lot of photos, both with digital cameras and with your mobile phone. Sharing those photos on Google+ is quite simple.

To share a photo:

**1** Make sure you're logged on to Google+.

**2** Click the box that contains the words 'Share what's new ...'.

**3** Enter a caption for your photo.

**4** Click the camera icon and click Add photos.

**5** Upload an image.

**6** Choose which circles to share with.

**7** Click Share.

**? DID YOU KNOW?**

You can also create a photo album and then organise your pictures there. Just click Create an album from the drop-down menu.

# Sharing a photo album on Google+

Sharing one photo at a time is good for some occasions, but at other times you'll want to share numerous pictures at once (such as from a recent holiday or birthday celebration). Google+ allows you to upload albums, which is a nice time-saving feature.

To share a photo album:

**1** Make sure you're logged on to Google+.

**2** Click the Photos icon in the top bar.

**3** Click Add New Photos.

**4** In the pop-up window that appears, you can drag photos or click Select photos from your computer.

**5** If you want, change the album name to something more descriptive than the current date.

**6** Click Create album.

**? DID YOU KNOW?**

You can view your own photo albums by clicking Your albums in the sidebar of the main photo gallery page.

# Viewing photos from your circle on Google+

Lots of people in your circles will be posting photos to Google+. Here's how you can look at them:

 **1** Make sure you're logged on to Google+.

**2** Click the Photos icon in the top bar.

**3** You'll see a view of photos from your circles.

**4** You can click a photo to zoom in and see comments.

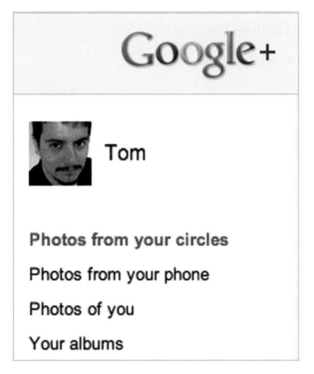

Google+

Tom

**Photos from your circles**

**Photos from your phone**

**Photos of you**

**Your albums**

# Sharing a video on Google+

Most of us have lots of videos of birthday parties, special events, holidays and other memories. Sharing those videos on Google+ is also very simple.

To share a video:

**1** Make sure you're logged on to Google+.

**2** Click the box that contains the words 'Share what's new ...'.

**3** Enter a caption for your video.

**4** Click the video icon and click Upload video or YouTube, depending on where the video is.

**5** Follow the prompts to share the video.

**6** Choose which circles to share with.

**7** Click Share.

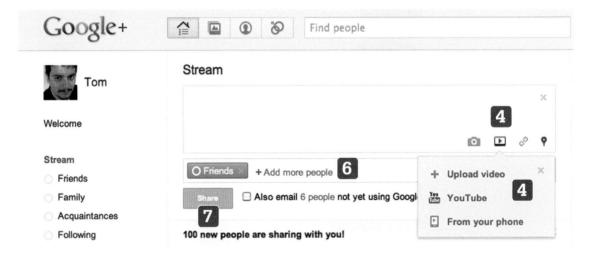

**? DID YOU KNOW?**

You can also share video and photos directly from your phone. Click From your phone to do that!

# Adding comments on Google+

Just like on Facebook, you can leave comments on anything anyone in your circles posts on Google+.

To post a comment:

**1** Make sure you're logged on to Google+.

**2** Find a post shared by another user.

**3** Click in the box that says 'Add a comment'.

**4** Add your comment and click Post comment.

now. The only place where I'm still stymied is using something like Seesmic web where you can scroll in every direction.

There have been a few wonky things that are natural in a newly released OS so I figure updates will be quick coming over the next few weeks.

9:13 AM

**4** That's good to know!

**4** Post comment    Cancel

Hide Comments

# Adding a +1 on Google+

If someone posts something you really like on Google+, you can 'like' it by giving it a +1.

To +1 a post:

**1** Make sure you're logged on to Google+.

**2** Find a post shared by another user that you like.

**3** Click the +1 button under the post.

# Muting a post on Google+

Sometimes you add a comment to a discussion on Google+ that will end up going on for days and days. Instead of suffering constant notifications when this happens, you can 'mute' a post.

To mute a post:

**1** Make sure you're logged on to Google+.

**2** Find the post you want to mute.

**3** Click the arrow icon in the upper right of the post.

**4** Select Mute this post from the menu.

Public **3** ⊙

Link to this post

Report abuse

**4** Mute this post

Block this person

**?** **DID YOU KNOW?**

Once you've muted a post, you will no longer see the post in your streams.

# Sharing on Google+

What if someone on Google+ shares a photo or video that you think people in your circles should see? On Google+ you can easily share anything posted by another user.

To share:

1. Make sure you're logged on to Google+.

2. Find a post created by another user.

3. Click the Share link under the post.

4. Add your own caption to the shared post.

5. Select which circles you will share the item with.

6. Click Share.

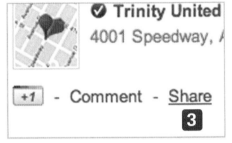

# Restrict sharing on Google+

What if you post something on Google+ and don't want others to repost? Google+ lets you restrict sharing:

1. Make sure you're logged on to Google+.

2. Find the post you want to restrict.

3. Click the arrow icon in the upper right of the post.

4. Select Disable reshare from the menu.

**3** ⊙

**Edit this post**

Delete this post

Disable comments

**4** Disable reshare

# Working with circles in Google+

Circles are how you keep everyone organised in Google+.

Whenever you post a status update, photo, video or link, you can choose which circles get to see what you've posted.

You can choose one or more circles, or post to the general public (these posts will be visible to the Internet at large). If you post to a circle, a person has to be in that circle in order to see it, so circles provide a greater degree of privacy.

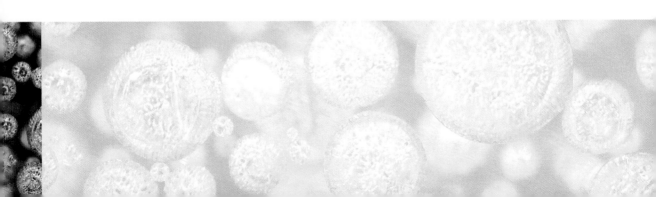

But how do you put people in circles? Simply click the Circles icon in the top navigation bar. You will see a screen where you can manage circles.

All you have to do is drag people into different circles to make them a member of that circle.

You can also hover over the Add to circles box by their name and then add them to whatever circles you've set up.

# Notifications in Google+

Along the right side of the top bar you'll notice a number right next to your name. Sometimes this number will be greater than 0 and be highlighted in red. This is your notifications bar.

When you click it, you'll see notes about people who have left a comment on a post you've made, +1'd (which is similar to like on Facebook) a post you've made, or put you in a circle.

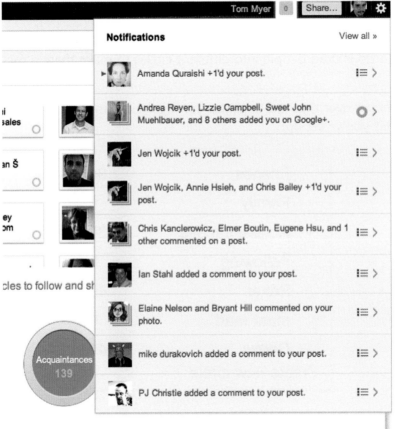

# Viewing a specific stream on Google+

Once you have your friends and colleagues organised into different circles, you can focus on one stream or another from any of those circles. For example, you may only want to see what your 'Friends' or your 'Work Colleagues' are talking about. The default mode for Google+ is to show you what everyone is posting.

To switch to a specific stream:

**1** Make sure you're logged on to Google+.

**2** In the left navigation bar, click the name of the stream you want to switch to.

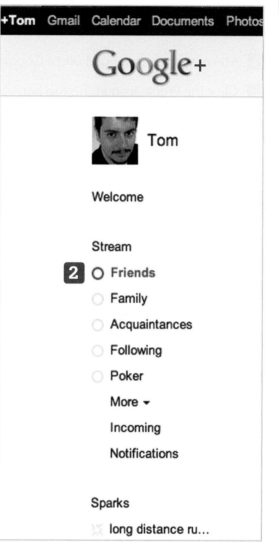

? **DID YOU KNOW?**
The Incoming stream is populated with stuff from people who aren't in your circles. It's a great way to discover people you may not know.

# Viewing your own profile on Google+

If you want to view your own profile on Google+:

**1** Make sure you're logged on to Google+.

**2** Click the Profile icon in the top bar.

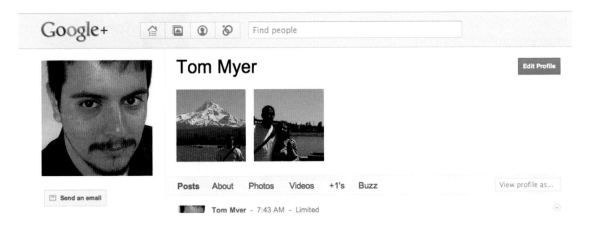

# Starting a hangout on Google+

One of the more interesting features on Google+ is the hangout, which is basically a way for up to 10 Google+ users to have a video chat. On Google+ you can create a hangout and then invite specific people or people from a circle to join that hangout.

To start a hangout:

**1** Make sure you're logged on to Google+.

**2** Click the Start a Hangout button in the right navigation pane.

**3** In the pop-up window that appears, you'll see that the video camera attached to your computer will start (you'll see your own face in a moment!).

**4** You can add participants to the hangout by choosing circles or inviting specific people.

**5** Click Hang out when you're ready to go.

**ALERT:** You must have a working video camera or webcam on your computer to start or join a hangout.

# Sparks on Google+

On Google+, a 'spark' is a feed on a topic that you can share with friends. You'd use sparks to keep track of different interests (such as sports, pastimes, hobbies, etc.). You can add individual sparks to your profile.

To create a spark:

**1** Make sure you're logged on to Google+.

**2** Click on Sparks in the left navigation pane.

**3** You'll see a list of popular sparks already there. To view any of these, simply click the image associated with a spark.

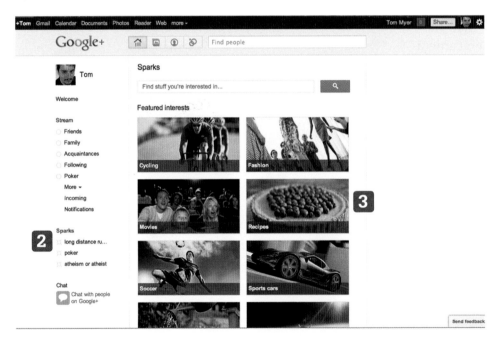

**? DID YOU KNOW?**

As of this writing, sparks are private. Nobody can see what sparks you've selected.

**4** You can also search for a specific spark by using the search feature.

**5** If you want to add a spark to your profile, click the Add interest button.

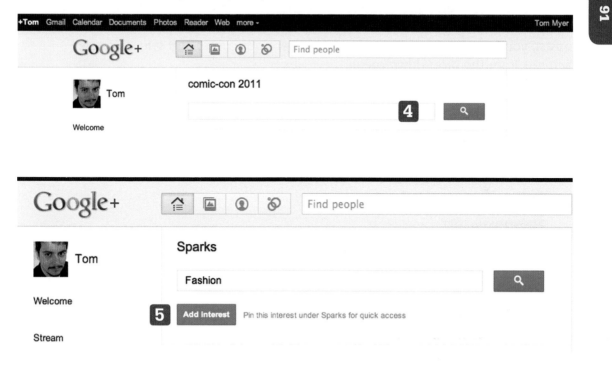

# Your Google+ settings

If at any time you wish to change your settings on Google+ (for example, some users complain that they get a lot of emails from Google+ when people comment on their posts), you can click the gear icon in the upper right corner and select Google+ Settings from the drop-down menu.

From that screen you can edit your notification settings and configure your privacy settings and other settings.

| Google accounts | | | |
|---|---|---|---|
| **Account overview** | | | |
| **Profile and privacy** | | | |
| **Google+** | **Google+** | | |
| **Language** | « Back to Google+ | | |
| **Data liberation** | | | |
| **Connected accounts** | **Set delivery preferences** | | |

**Email**   myerman@gmail.com

**Phone**   ▾ Add phone number

via   ⦿ Push notifications   ○ Don't notify me

**Receive notifications**
Get notified by email or SMS when someone...

| Posts and mentions of my name | Email | Phone |
|---|---|---|
| Mentions me in a post | ☐ | ☑ |
| Shares a post with me directly | ☐ | ☑ |
| Comments on a post I created | ☐ | ☑ |
| Comments on a post after I comment on it | ☐ | ☐ |
| **Circles** | Email | Phone |
| Adds me to a circle | ☐ | ☐ |
| **Photos of me** | Email | Phone |
| Wants to tag me in a photo | ☐ | ☐ |
| Tags me in a photo | ☐ | ☑ |
| Comments on a photo after I comment on it | ☐ | ☐ |
| Comments on a photo I am tagged in | ☐ | ☐ |

# 6 Blogging

| | |
|---|---|
| Starting your own blog | 96 |
| Finding quality blogs | 97 |
| Before you start a blog | 99 |
| Nine ideas for keeping your blog going | 101 |
| Start blogging with Tumblr | 102 |
| Start blogging with Posterous | 103 |
| Start blogging with Blogger | 105 |
| Start blogging with WordPress.com | 110 |

# Introduction

So what is a blog? Technically speaking, a blog is a type of web site, usually maintained by one or more individuals, with regular diary-like entries, photo galleries, videos, or commentary on current events or even other blogs. Blogs can and usually do contain features that allow readers to leave comments or share individual blog posts on Twitter, Facebook and other social networking sites.

Most blogs are focused on just one topic, or a series of tightly related topics. For example, my blog cognito ergo myerman (at http://www.myerman.com) typically focuses on my adventures in technology and writing, but every once in a while I'll throw in a piece about marathon training, wearing kilts or some other topic that takes my fancy.

## COGITO ERGO MYERMAN

writing. running. coding. snarking.

ABOUT ME

BOOKS

FLICKR

@MYERMAN

GET OFF MY LAWN

TRIPLE DOG DARE MEDIA

### KILTS AND KLOUT

I hope everyone who attended SxSW Interactive 2011 had as much fun as I did. I had a blast as one of the #5kilts guys (for a little taste of the insanity, check out the 5 Kilts KeepStream that Alex Jones set up at http://keepstream.com/BaldMan/5kilts).

To summarize, we walked around in kilts, took lots of pictures with people, got interviewed a lot (CNN, GenConnect.com, Maxim Magazine, Karma Movement, you name it), got to hang out with Stella the Tito's Vodka Spokesmutt, played Live Angry Birds with the kilts on, and danced backup to Jen Wojcik and Kate Buck of Pinqued during Tech Karaoke.

It turns out that if you have 4-5 guys in kilts walking down the street, people want to approach them and talk. Sometimes the talk is all about "what are you wearing under the kilt?" ("my boots!") but other times these encounters led to some interesting conversations and connections.

In other words, we had a good time, didn't get arrested, and our stuff was retweeted on Twitter or shared on Facebook about 1000 times in the course of 5 days of insane shenanigans. Although only one of the kilted guys (Simon Salt) has marketing bona fides, I'd say we did pretty good at attracting attention for our daily sponsors--not bad for a stunt that went horribly right.

Why do I mention all of this? Well, because I've been thinking a lot about influence

One of the world's biggest blogs is The Huffington Post, with many contributors writing on politics, business, entertainment, technology, lifestyle, media and other topics. It's so big that you'd probably categorise it as an online newspaper, as it has US, UK and Canada editions.

In fact, many large traditional newspapers, such as the *Guardian*, also have blogs as part of their online presence. These blogs allow greater reader interaction with the writers and the story.

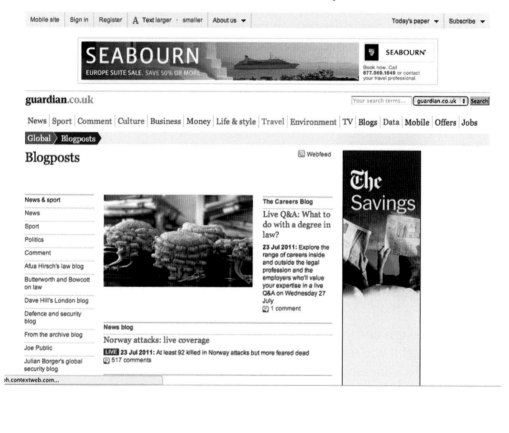

# Starting your own blog

If you do a quick Google search of 'blogs' you could end up going through a list of many millions of blogs in topics ranging from technology and gardening to politics and cooking and everything in between. It seems that just about everyone in the world has started a blog on every conceivable topic.

So why start your own blog? There are a great number of reasons for doing so, but they can mostly be grouped into one of these major areas:

1. You have a particular voice or point of view that isn't being expressed. For example, you may feel that a particular take on politics or world affairs isn't to your liking, or that participants in the conversation are missing a valid point. Or you might just want to have a soapbox for your opinions.

2. You have experience in a particular area that you wish to share. For example, you may be a master gunsmith, an avid hunter, a miracle worker with tomato plants or an experienced mountain climber. Offering your expertise to the world is a very valid reason for starting a blog, no matter how many other experts there might be who share your knowledge.

3. You want to share a passion or hobby. For example, if you're an avid photographer and world traveller with an extensive collection of wildlife you've photographed around the world, sharing these photos is a great way to enter the world of blogging.

4. You may want to let people know about the area you live in now. Creating a 'destination' blog that showcases your home town, complete with video tours, photography and write-ups of local landmarks or historical monuments, is a great reason to start a blog.

5. You own a business and you want to share what you do for a living with the world. It doesn't matter if you're a master furniture maker, a glassblower or a software developer – there are aspects of your job that others (and not just your customers) might find interesting.

6. You want to keep track of a personal goal and share your progress with others. For example, many people have used blogs as a daily diary of their weight-loss or fitness programmes.

# Finding quality blogs

Okay, so you've convinced yourself that you want to start a blog, and that maybe, just maybe, you might have something worthwhile to share with others.

The next question becomes, where do I find quality blogs on the Internet? Sure, there might be several million out there, and maybe even several thousand just devoted to your topic (be it kite-flying or cooking pasta), but you probably want to see what others are doing first.

Why? Mostly because it's always a good idea to see what others are talking about, just as a way to get you inspired. Another good reason to do this is so you can start reaching out to these other bloggers and become a part of their community.

A great place to start is http://www.google.com/blogsearch. The search interface is very much like Google's main search screen, but the results are limited to blogs.

---

Google
blogs

| marathons | Search |

About Google

© 2011 - Privacy

---

A simpler approach is to run a regular Google search and then add +blog to your search query. This will return a list of blogs that match your search query.

Google

marathon +blog

About 68,300,000 results (0.25 seconds)

Advanced search

Everything

Images

Videos

News

Shopping

More

Austin, TX 78727
Change location

Show search tools

▶ **Mizz Duffy's Marathon Blog**
mrsduffysmarathonblog.blogspot.com/ - Cached
2 days ago – Not only did you overpay for a pool swim and a cramped double-loop bike course that doesn't even count as a **marathon** qualifier*, ...

**Mike's Marathon Blog**
mikesmarathonblog.com/ - Cached
2 days ago – Yes, Jacky was lying in the bed next to me in excruciating pain, but this is **Mike's Marathon Blog**, not Jacky's. I can't speak for her! ...

Boston **Marathon** blog - News from the Boston Globe - Boston.com
www.boston.com/sports/**marathon**/**blog**/ - Cached
Apr 19, 2011 – Boston **Marathon** news and commentary from the sports writers of the Boston Globe.

New York City **Marathon** - On the Run **Blog** - NYTimes.com
**marathon.blogs.nytimes.com**/ - Cached
Apr 20, 2011 – The New York Times provides coverage of the New York City **Marathon**, scheduled for Nov. 7, including news, features and advice for runners.

The Get Your Serenity **Blog**
www.getyourserenity.com/ - Cached
I haven't been good at writing in my **blog** in recent weeks, but I couldn't ... just like when I was doing **marathons**... after I figured that out, it was time to ...

**Marathon Pundit**
marathonpundit.blogspot.com/ - Cached
3 hours ago – Today a US Chamber of Commerce **blog** points to the unconstitutionality of a long-rumored proposed Obama executive order that will force ...

Lindsay's Half-**Marathon Blog**
lindsayshalfmarathon.wordpress.com/ - Cached
Jun 3, 2009 – I also learned that I do not have a passion for updating this **blog**. Without

mrsduffysmarathonblog.blogspot.com

photos! SDC10953 With Dad. ...

# Before you start a blog

Before starting a blog, you need to consider the following:

**1** Put together a general outline of what you want to talk about. You don't have to stick to one topic, but it's usually easier if you know what your 'beat' is going to be. On newspapers, journalists have beats, topics they focus on (such as sports, crime, business and so on). Knowing what your beat is will make your blogging a lot easier.

**2** Take some time to read over what others are writing about on similar blogs. Are they missing certain topics or viewpoints? Do you disagree with any of the bloggers? A good way to get started on a blog is in response to another blog (that doesn't mean you have to be mean or vindictive with your blogging – see below).

**3** Take the time to comment on other blogs. Let people know who you are and that you're out there. This will help drive traffic back to your own blog, but also it's the social thing to do – say hi, even if you disagree with me. Keep it civil, as you're a guest in someone else's house!

**4** Work out how often you want to post updates. Will it be every day? Once a week? Twice a week? Once a month? You need to have some kind of regularity when it comes to publishing posts, and different audiences are willing to put up with different frequencies. There are plenty of bloggers who post numerous times a day.

**5** Figure out what your tone is going to be. Will it be humorous, sarcastic, scholarly? It doesn't really matter, but establishing a tone will help set your blog apart.

**6** You'll also need to have some kind of policy for handling comments. A great many of the comments you'll get on your blog will be from friends, colleagues and family, but you'll occasionally get people who leave nasty remarks. Do you publish those? Ignore them? Delete them? Respond to them? It's up to you.

**7** Another thing to think about is the mix of content types you're going to publish on your blog. Yes, it's probably pretty easy to write blog posts, but you also have access to video, photography, audio files and so on. Don't limit yourself!

8 How are you going to get the word out about your blog? A lot of people will blog and then tell their friends on Twitter, Facebook and Google+ about their newest blog posts. Others will use email. Again, it's up to you.

9 Finally, choose what platform you want to blog on. In this book I'll talk about different blogging platforms (Tumblr, Posterous, Blogger, WordPress.com) but it's also possible to host your own WordPress site (for example) if you have the expertise and time to get that set up.

# Nine ideas for keeping your blog going

It's really easy to run out of ideas when you start a blog, so here are a few ideas for stoking the creative fires:

**1**  For your first blog post, it's a good idea to introduce who you are, what you're all about, some of your interests, and what this blog is going to be about.

**2**  Write a blog post about current events, either in the general news section, or something that is happening in your local region, or in your area of expertise.

**3**  Write a blog post in response to someone else's blog post, then tell that person about it so you can have a two-way conversation about the issue.

**4**  Liveblog an event, such as a seminar, a speech, a town council meeting, or any other gathering of people you think are discussing interesting things.

**5**  Create a short video presentation or tutorial that introduces a visitor to your topic of interest. For example, if you're a carpenter, a quick video tutorial on how to use different tools would be an excellent addition to your blog on carpentry.

**6**  Interview an expert in your field and publish it to your blog.

**7**  Summarise the 'best of' or 'top 10' in your area of expertise. If you have a blog on acting, maybe the top 10 male British actors of the 20th century. Or if you're a movie blogger, the top 10 action movies of the past 5 years.

**8**  Share what you're reading right now. Your blog post can be about a fiction or non-fiction book. Provide your thoughts or viewpoints on the book.

**9**  Ask a question or ask for an opinion. Make sure that people can easily add comments in response to what you've posted. For example, you might ask, on a travel blog, what readers' favourite destinations are in Europe. Or if you're a fitness blogger, what people's favourite winter exercises are.

# Start blogging with Tumblr

An easy way to get started quickly is to use a service like Tumblr. Tumblr allows you to create a special-interest blog on its servers within minutes.

To create a Tumblr:

1. Open your web browser and visit http://www.tumblr.com.

2. Enter your email address, a password and a URL for your Tumblr. For example, if you want to start a blog about hang gliding in Scotland, your Tumblr address might be scotlandHangGliding.Tumblr.com. If instead you want to blog about French fashion, try frenchFashion.Tumblr.com.

3. If your Tumblr URL hasn't already been taken, you'll be approved within seconds. You should see a confirmation screen that prompts you to add your first blog post.

**HOT TIP:** Once you've got your first blog post up and running, share a link to that blog post on Twitter and Facebook!

# Start blogging with Posterous

Posterous is another quick and easy blogging platform. It's free to sign up, and once you're set up you can simply send emails to a posterous.com email address to blog. Don't worry, though, as you can tell Posterous only to allow emails from certain addresses, or that you have to approve all posts before they go live.

The great thing about Posterous is that you can attach photos, videos and documents to your emails and the service will convert them to the proper attachments for your blog. For example, if you attach three photos to your blog post about your latest trip to Paris, Posterous will automatically create a photo gallery of your attachments.

To create a Posterous blog:

1. Point your web browser at http://www.posterous.com.

2. On the home page you'll see a sign-up form.

3. Enter your email, a username and a password.

4. Your username can be anything you like. The username becomes part of the web address for your blog. For example, if your username is kiteflyingexpert, your posterous address would be http://kiteflyingexpert.posterous. com.

5. You'll receive an email when you sign up to confirm that you've set up a Posterous blogging account.

**DID YOU KNOW?**

My Posterous blog is http://myerman.posterous.com. I write about technology, poker, marathon training and writing. Drop by and say hi!

6 Once you've registered, you can create blog posts by sending an email to the Posterous email address assigned to your blog.

7 You also have access to an admin panel where you can edit posts, select a theme for your blog, and more.

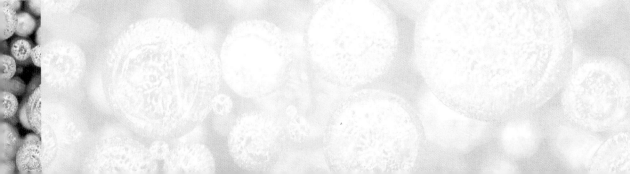

# Start blogging with Blogger

Another extremely popular blogging platform is Blogger, which is owned by Google. You can easily sign up for a Blogger account by going to http://blogger.com and registering there.

**1** Once you've successfully registered, you're redirected to the Blogger Dashboard. To create your first blog, click Create Your Blog Now.

2 On the next screen, give your new blog a title and an address. You'll have to check the availability of your address before you can create the blog.

**3** Next, choose a starter template.

4 As soon as you do that, you're free to start blogging! Use the editor to create your first post and click Publish Post when you're happy with it.

Blogger comes with a whole set of WYSIWYG tools that help you create blog posts without having to know HTML.

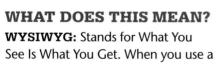

# Start blogging with WordPress.com

Although you can create your own site and install the WordPress software directly on it, you need to have some level of expertise to do that – particularly when the time comes to install the database. You may or may not have the time to do that, or have a hosting account that supports MySQL and PHP.

Of course, if you want to blog with WordPress, all you have to do is go over to WordPress.com and click Get started here. This will start the process of creating a hosted blog on that site. In this regard, your WordPress.com site will be similar to a blog you create on Tumblr or Blogger.

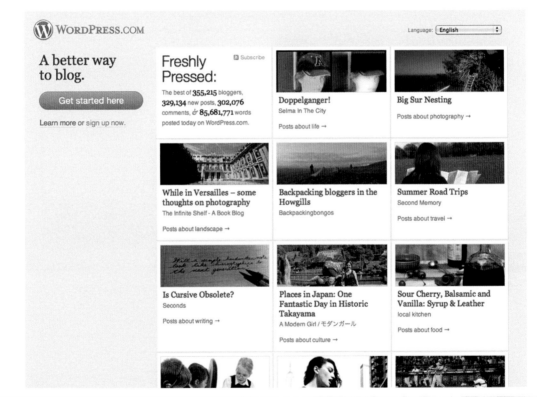

**1** Fill out the form, providing WordPress with an address for your site, a username, password and email address.

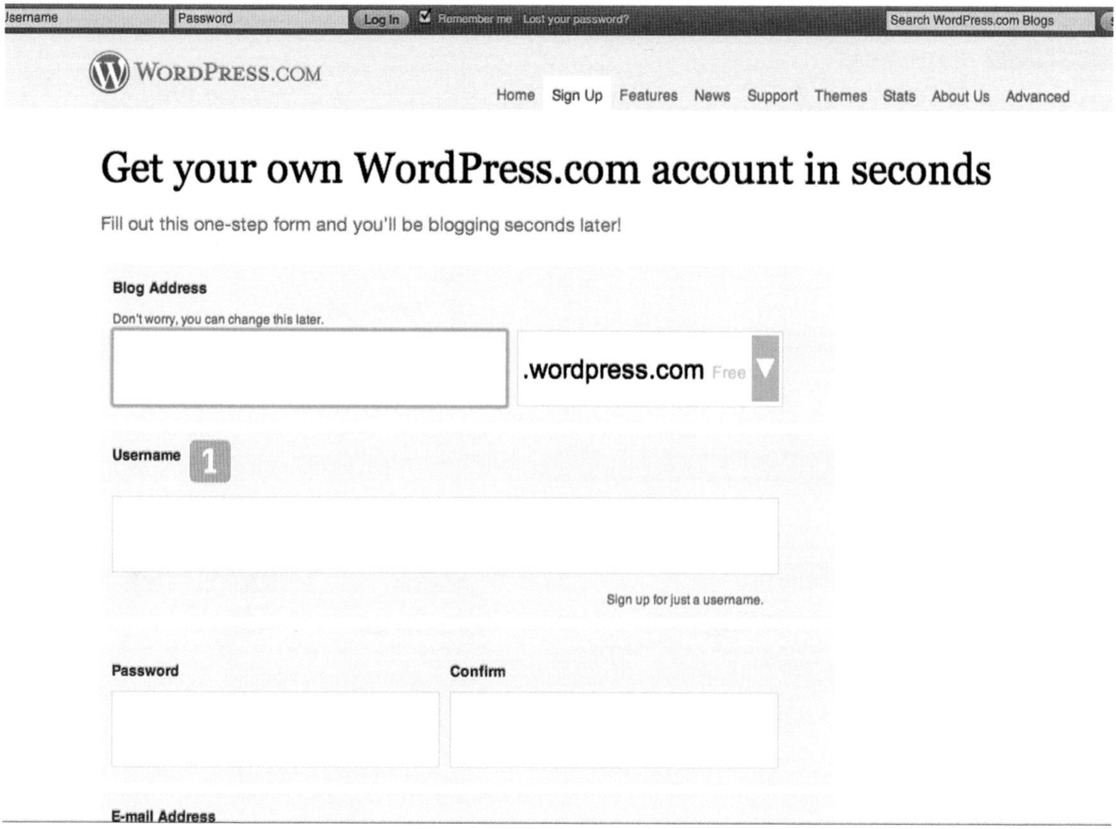

Username | Password | Log In | ☑ Remember me | Lost your password? | Search WordPress.com Blogs

**WORDPRESS.COM**

Home  Sign Up  Features  News  Support  Themes  Stats  About Us  Advanced

# Get your own WordPress.com account in seconds

Fill out this one-step form and you'll be blogging seconds later!

**Blog Address**

Don't worry, you can change this later.

[                    ]  .wordpress.com  Free ▼

**Username** [1]

[                                        ]

Sign up for just a username.

**Password**                **Confirm**

[            ]              [            ]

**E-mail Address**

2 Once you've registered, you can visit the dashboard. Use the QuickPress feature to start blogging.

# 7 Photos and video

Introduction to Flickr                                    115

Create a Flickr account                                   116

Upload an image to Flickr                                 117

Organise images into sets                                 119

Search for images                                         124

Connect with people on Flickr                             126

Introduction to Instagram                                 127

Downloading the application                               128

Taking a picture with Instagram                           129

Finding friends on Instagram                              131

Introduction to YouTube                                   132

Searching for and watching videos on YouTube             133

Signing up for YouTube                                    134

Uploading your first video                                135

Subscribing to a channel on YouTube                       138

Introduction to Vimeo                                     139

Signing up for Vimeo                                      140

Uploading a video                                         142

Exploring Vimeo                                           143

# Introduction

So far I've talked a great deal about Twitter, Facebook, Google+ and blogging, and in each case I've mentioned the power of photography and video. On Facebook and other social networks, people will share photos and videos that they've taken with their phones just minutes previously. On blogs all across the Web, photos and videos are used to illustrate blog posts or as the main attractions of the blogs themselves.

In this chapter, I'll concentrate more of my attention on the social media sites that are focused strictly on photographic and video content.

The services we'll cover are:

- Flickr
- Instagram
- YouTube
- Vimeo.

© by Toyokazu

**Upload**
More ways to get your photos online.

Multiple ways to upload your photos to Flickr—through the web, your mobile device, email or your favorite photo applications.

**Discover**
See what's going on in your world.

Keep up with your friends and share your stories with comments & notes. Add rich information like tags, locations & people.

**Share**
Your photos are everywhere you are.

Upload your photos once to Flickr, then easily and safely share them through Facebook, Twitter, email, blogs and more.

Sign up now  Free!

It takes less than a minute to create your free account & start sharing!
Have a Google or Facebook account? You can use them to sign in!

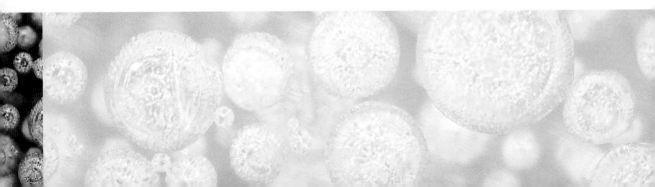

# Introduction to Flickr

Flickr is one of the best online photo management and sharing web sites out there. If you visit Flickr.com you will see that millions of people have signed up for an account and are sharing all kinds of photographs, ranging from snapshots of their kid's birthday party to professional travel photography of the Hindu Kush mountains, and everything in between.

Flickr's mission is twofold:

- Allow people to upload and organise their photos. With Flickr you can create sets of photos, and you can tag your photos with different keywords. Other Flickr users are free to create galleries of photos that make sense to them, incorporating photos from many different users.

- Allow users to share photos with the people in their lives. Because of this, you can upload images from your laptop or desktop computer, directly from your cameraphone, or through other services (like Instagram, more on them later).

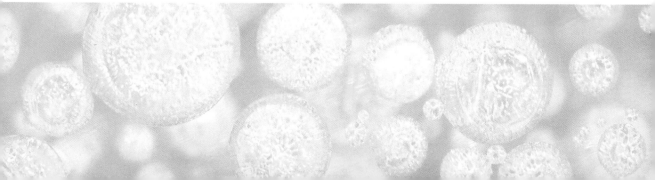

# Create a Flickr account

To create a Flickr account, follow these steps:

**1** Point your browser at http://www.flickr.com.

**2** Click Sign Up Now.

**3** In the pop-up window, you have various choices for creating an account.

- You can sign in with your Yahoo account (if you have one).
- You can sign in with your Facebook account credentials.
- You can sign in with your Google account credentials.
- You can create a new account.

**4** Once you've signed in or created a new account, you'll see your dashboard.

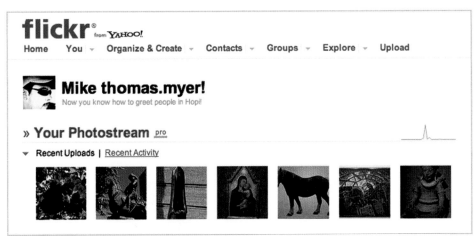

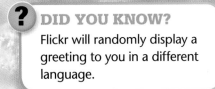

**DID YOU KNOW?**

Flickr will randomly display a greeting to you in a different language.

# Upload an image to Flickr

There are various ways of adding an image to Flickr, but the easiest is via the web site.

To upload an image:

**1** Make sure you're logged into Flickr.

**2** On the right-hand side of your dashboard, click Upload Photos and Video.

**3** On the next screen, click Choose photos and videos.

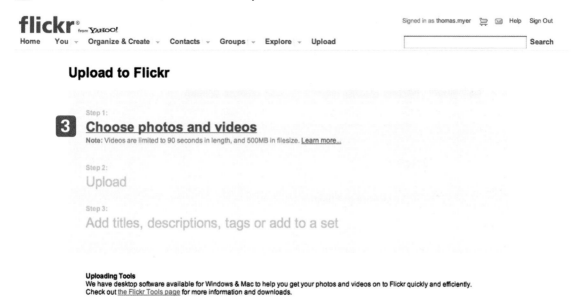

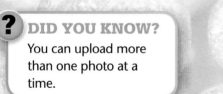

**? DID YOU KNOW?**
You can upload more than one photo at a time.

**? DID YOU KNOW?**
It's a good idea to attach tags to images when you upload them.

**4** Select a photo from your computer's hard drive.

**5** Set your privacy settings for your image and click Upload Photos and Videos.

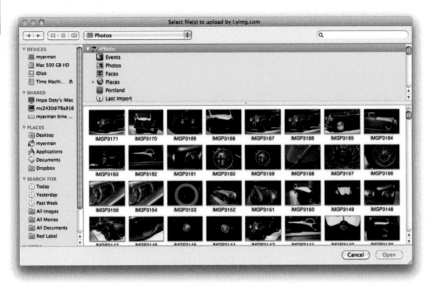

## WHAT DOES THIS MEAN?

**Tag:** A descriptive keyword, usually one word, that helps to describe an image. Tags help search engines like the one on Flickr do their jobs better.

# Organise images into sets

After you've uploaded various images on to Flickr, you'll need to organise them. The best way to organise your images is to use sets.

To create a set on Flickr:

**1** Make sure you're logged into Flickr.

**2** Click Batch Organize in the main navigation bar along the top.

**3** You'll see an empty workspace with instructions on it for dragging pictures. The pictures you've uploaded are along the bottom.

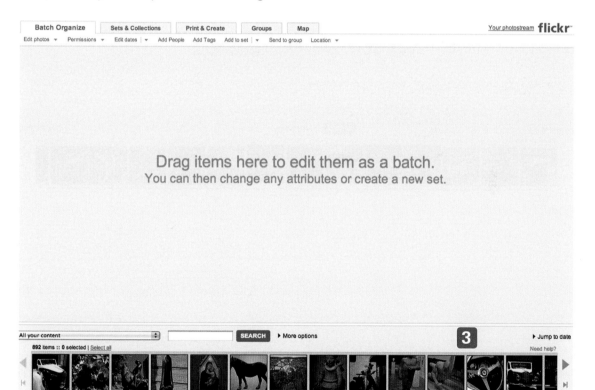

**4** Select one or more images below and drag them into the workspace.

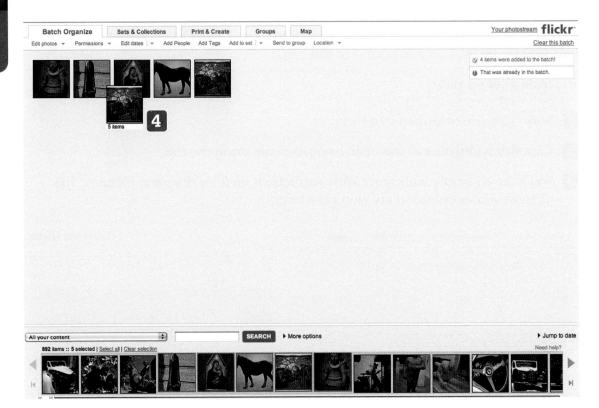

**5** The Batch Organize tab should be active. To assign these images to a set, click Add to set and choose either New set or Existing set, depending on the circumstances.

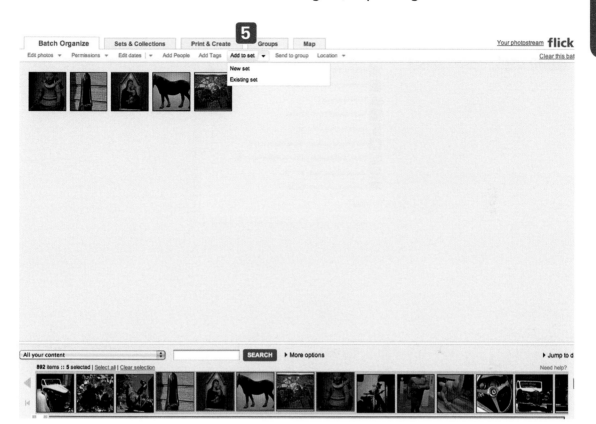

**6** If it's an existing set, choose a set from one of the ones you've created.

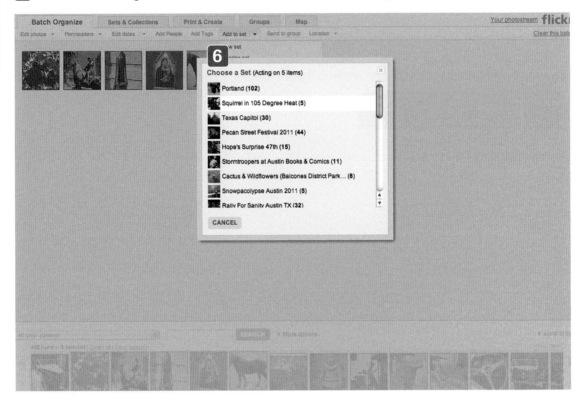

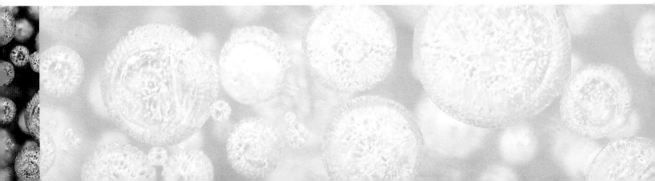

**7** If it's a new set, you'll be shown a page where you can enter a name for the set and then save your work.

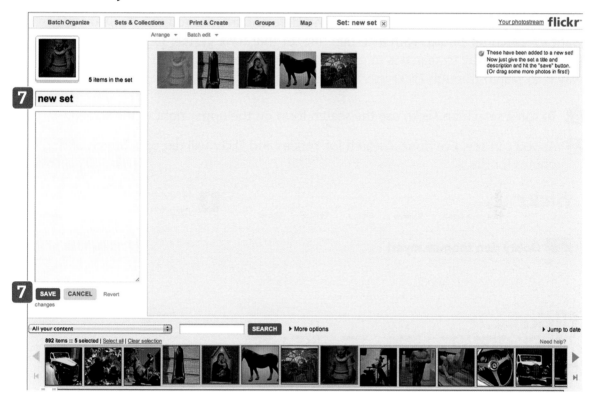

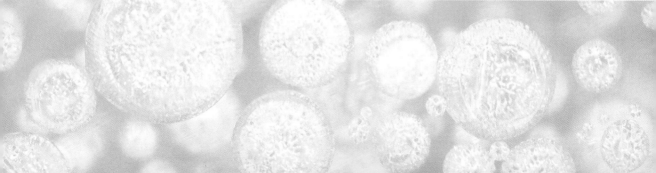

# Search for images

Flickr allows users to search for photos using different criteria. You may, for example, want to search for photos with a certain title, or that have certain tags attached to them. Another way to search is to explore Flickr's 'interestingness' archives. Still another way is to search through Flickr user groups devoted to your subject.

**1** To run a search on Flickr, use the search form on the upper right of the screen.

**2** As you can see, I've done a search for Yorkies and Flickr will dig up a bunch of dog photos for me.

**flickr** from YAHOO!
Home　You ▾　Organize & Create ▾　Contacts ▾　Groups ▾　Explore ▾　Upload

**1** Signed in as thomas.myer　🛒 ✉ Help　Sign Out
yorkie　　　　　　Search

**Dobrý den thomas.myer!**
Now you know how to greet people in Czech!

**flickr** from YAHOO!
Home　You ▾　Organize & Create ▾　Contacts ▾　Groups ▾　Explore ▾　Upload

Signed in as thomas.myer　🛒 ✉ Help　Sign

**Search**　　Photos | Groups | People
[ Everyone's Uploads ▾ ]　yorkie **2**　　　　　[ SEARCH ]　Full Text | Tags Only
　　　　　　　　　　　　　　　　　　　　　　Advanced Search

**3** I can sort this result set by relevance, recency and interestingness. I can also choose to see how big the thumbnails are.

**4** If I sort on Interesting and switch over to medium thumbnails, I get a different set of images.

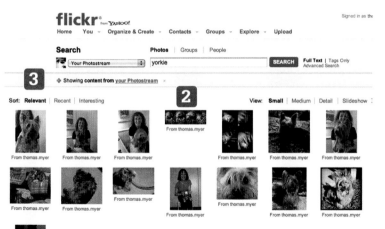

**5** To view an individual image, click on it and see a detail view.

Sun Yorkie

# Connect with people on Flickr

The best way to connect with people on Flickr is to leave comments on their photos. However, you can also send Flickr users private messages.

To send someone a private message:

**1** Make sure you're logged into Flickr.

**2** When you've found an image you like and you want to contact the photographer, click the envelope icon next to the image name.

**3** A new window will open, prompting you to write a message. Fill in a subject and a message body and click Send This.

Subject:

**3**

PREVIEW or SEND THIS

Or, return to your message list.

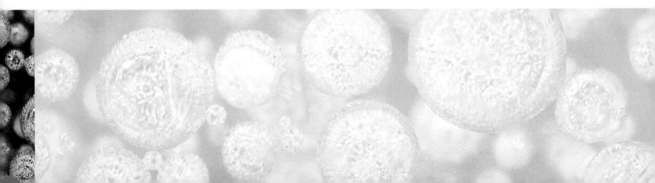

# Introduction to Instagram

What is Instagram? It's an iPhone app that allows photographers to post photos directly to the Instagram social network and other networks like Facebook, Twitter and even Flickr.

What makes Instagram different from other services like Flickr? Where Flickr really excels at offering incredibly robust tools for organising and sharing all your photos, Instagram is really about having a lot of fun with your photography. With Instagram, you take a picture, apply a filter and post your work of art for others to see.

The filters are what makes Instagram fun – you can apply wild colours, retro black and white, and weird borders that turn everyday images into works of art.

There's more: I've created a Flickr set of some of my favourite Instagram shots. They're available here: http://bit.ly/oyr1tW.

# Downloading the application

To get started with Instagram, turn on your iPhone and open the App Store.

Once you're in the store, do a search for Instagram.

Click Install and wait for the application to download and install. Once it's installed, you'll be asked to register with the service – don't worry, it's free.

When you first open the application, you won't see any images from anyone (you haven't made any friends yet!) but at some point, when you have connected with people, you'll see a stream of their photos.

What you can do right away is see the popular photos. Simply click on Popular and you'll see a list of the most commented and favourited photos on Instagram at the moment.

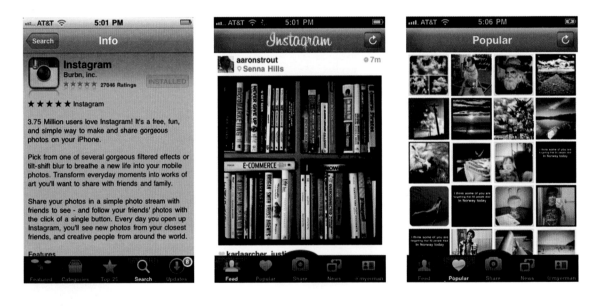

# Taking a picture with Instagram

Okay, it's time to take your first picture with Instagram. Along the bottom you'll notice a fairly big button labelled Share. Tap that button.

You can either take a picture with the iPhone's camera or choose an image from the photo library on the phone. For the purposes of this book, I've decided to choose a picture of a lovely statue I saw recently on a visit to a museum.

Once you've chosen or taken a photo, you can move and scale that image as you desire.

The next step is to add tilt shift, if you like. Instagram supports two types of tilt shifting: circular (or radial) and rectangular.

For example, here's an example of a rectangular tilt shift:

---

**WHAT DOES THIS MEAN?**

**Tilt shift:** Refers to digitally focusing on one part of your photo, creating more visual interest in the region that you've accentuated.

Notice that only those parts of the photograph inside the focus area are in focus. Everything else is blurred out. You can control the blurring effect with the slider.

Here's an example of a circular or radial tilt shift:

I've decided that I like the radial tilt shift better, so I apply that.

Next, I can choose from a variety of different filters. Since the filters change periodically and they are a lot of fun to play with, I'll leave it up to you to experiment. Here are a few choices side by side that I experimented with:

After settling on a filter, I can give my photograph a title and choose to share the image with my different social networks. When I'm ready, I click Done.

The final result is this:

# Finding friends on Instagram

Because Instagram is a social network, there's no point being on it unless you have some friends to share images back and forth with. Happily, Instagram has made it very easy to find friends and connect with them.

To find friends on Instagram:

**1** Click your username in the bottom toolbar and then tap Find Friends in the menu.

**2** On the next panel, you can find friends in these ways:
- From your own contact list.
- By connecting Instagram to Facebook and importing your friends there.
- By connecting Instagram to Twitter and importing your friends there.
- By doing a search of people already on Instagram.
- You can also tap on suggested users to see who is out there that might be worth following.

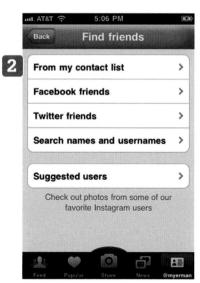

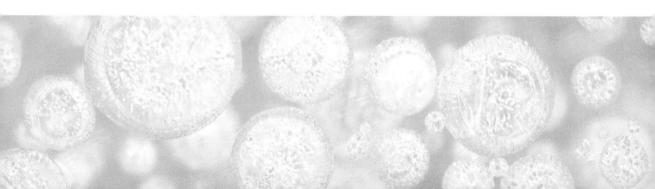

# Introduction to YouTube

YouTube is probably the world's most famous video-sharing site. It was launched in February 2005 (and later bought by Google) and allows people to discover literally hundreds of millions of films created and uploaded to its site.

What kinds of films? Everything from clips of feature films and TV shows to music videos to the creations of people using nothing more than the video cameras on their iPhones or Android phones.

Typically, when you sign up, you can upload videos up to 10 minutes in length and then share with your friends. There aren't a lot of restrictions on content (you have to own the copyright, of course), and just a quick look through YouTube's archives will give you an insight into the many thousands of categories already out there.

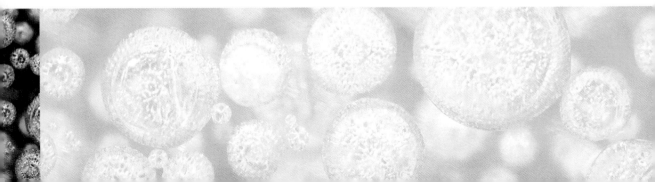

# Searching for and watching videos on YouTube

You don't have to become a member of YouTube to enjoy any of the content. To search for a video on YouTube:

 **1** Point your browser at www.youtube.com.

**2** Click Browse if you want to see popular videos.

**3** You can also click on Music, Shows, Trailers and Live to see videos in those categories.

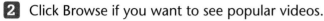

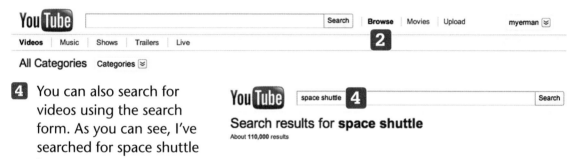

**4** You can also search for videos using the search form. As you can see, I've searched for space shuttle here.

**5** To view a video, click on the video's name or thumbnail.

# Signing up for YouTube

If you want to upload any of your own videos, you'll need to register with YouTube. The process is free and relatively painless.

To sign up for YouTube:

**1** Point your browser at the following address: www.youtube.com/signup.

**2** Fill out the form, entering an email address, a username (subject to availability), your location and other information like your date of birth and gender.

**3** Make sure that you understand the terms of service.

**4** Click I accept.

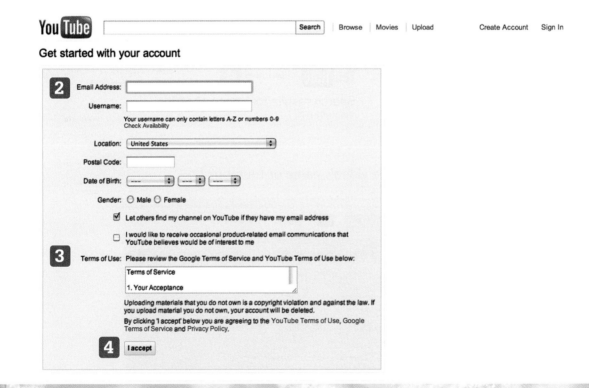

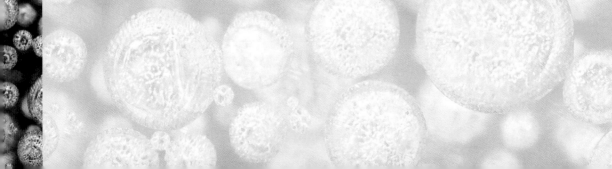

# Uploading your first video

Once you've created an account, uploading your first video is very easy.

**1** Make sure you're logged into YouTube.

**2** Click the Upload link in the top navigation bar.

**3** You can either upload a video or ...

**4** Record from webcam or ...

**5** Drag and drop video files directly on the page.

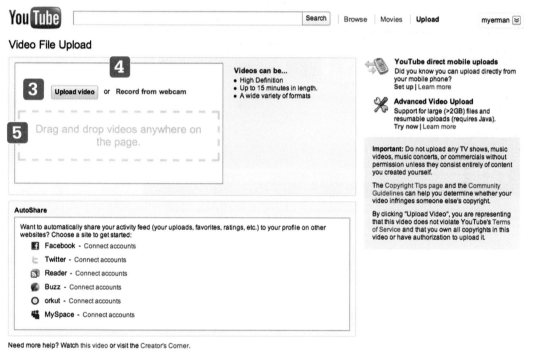

**6** For our purposes here, click Record Video from Webcam.

**7** You can now create your first video directly in YouTube. Just click Ready to Record when you're ready.

**8** Click the stop button in the lower left corner when you've stopped recording video.

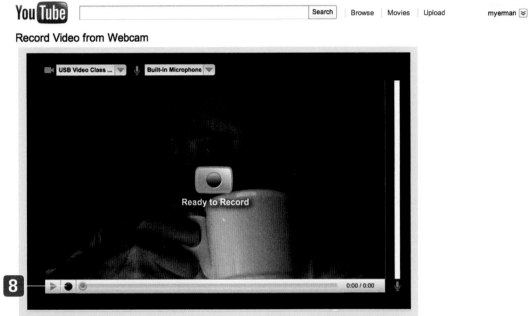

Use the tool to record a YouTube video instantly via your computer's webcam. For more details, please see here.Make sure your webcam is installed and working correctly.
Did you mean to upload an existing video from your computer?

Help    About    Press & Blogs    Copyright    Creators & Partners    Advertising    Developers    Safety    Privacy    Terms
Report a bug    Try something new!    Language: English    Location: Worldwide    Safety mode: Off

9 You can now preview your video, re-record it if you don't like what you see, or publish.

10 Once you've published it, you can add metadata to the video. For example, you can add a custom title, change the category the video is in, add location data to it and make it a private video if you like.

# Subscribing to a channel on YouTube

Many YouTube users have their own channels, where they regularly upload videos. Some of the users are quite busy, uploading several videos every day. Because YouTube knows you're busy, they let you subscribe to channels that you like. When you subscribe to a channel, you can get notifications that will tell you when a channel has been updated.

To subscribe to a channel:

**1** Make sure you're logged into YouTube.

**2** When you find a channel that you like, click the Subscribe button (it's usually by the channel owner's name). In the example below, my friend Stephanie Wonderlin has a great social media-related channel on YouTube called Tweetheart TV.

**3** When you subscribe, you get a notice from YouTube saying what your status is. Now every time you visit YouTube.com you will see a notice if there's new content for you to watch. You can also tick a box if you want an email notification.

# Introduction to Vimeo

If you're looking for high-quality video, or want to share your most creative work and get constructive feedback, then the best place for you isn't necessarily YouTube – it's Vimeo.

Vimeo is a community of highly creative film makers who really care about their craft. It was founded in 2004 by film enthusiasts and offers a safe haven for those who want to share their work in the digital video medium.

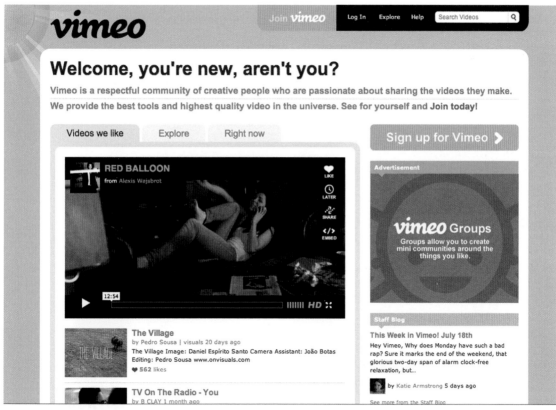

# Signing up for Vimeo

Signing up for Vimeo is really easy.

**1** Point your browser to vimeo.com.

**2** Click the Join Now button in the top navigation bar.

**3** You can join as a basic member for free. Click Basic.

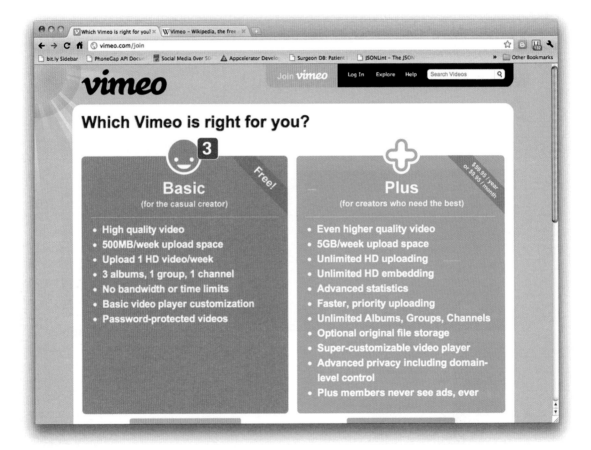

! **ALERT:** Before you can upload any video, you'll need to click the confirmation link that Vimeo will send to your email address.

4 Enter your first and last names, an email address and a password.

5 Agree to the terms of service and click Join Vimeo.

6 The first time you log into Vimeo, you'll see a Welcome screen that reminds you what you can and can't upload and what the limits are on your account.

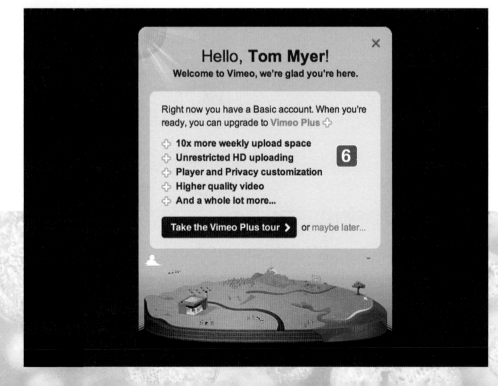

# Uploading a video

Now that you're a registered member, you can upload a video to Vimeo.

To upload a video:

**1** Click Upload a video.

**2** Click Choose a file to upload.

**3** Select a file from your computer's hard drive. It will start uploading. While you wait for that to complete, enter a title, description and keywords for your video.

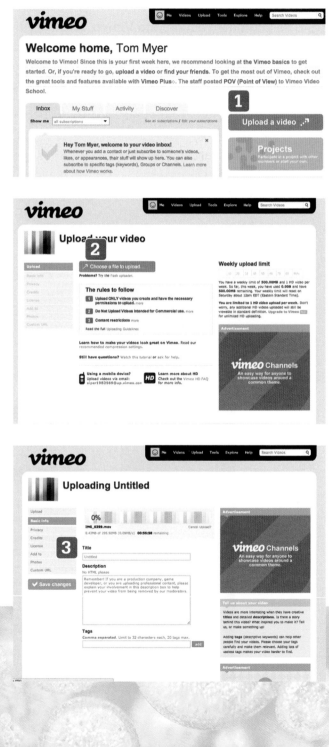

# Exploring Vimeo

While you're a member of Vimeo, it's a good idea to explore some of what the site has to offer. To start exploring, click the Explore link in the top navigation bar.

If you want to learn more about making good videos, click the Video School link. This part of the site features a number of tutorials that will make you a better video creator. The Video 101 article contains lots of great tips for the beginner.

If you want to see what others have created, click on Channels. A channel on Vimeo is a simple and easy way to showcase a series of videos.

Click on a channel to see what videos are available. Below I've clicked on the DSLR Photography School channel, and I see that it includes a variety of videos that will improve my digital SLR photography.

Click the Everywhere tab to learn more about streaming Vimeo to other devices: your mobile phone, streaming players, your TV and more.

# 8 Music

Introduction to Last.fm                              147

Starting a Last.fm profile                           148

Get music recommendations from Last.fm               149

Downloading the Last.fm Scrobbler                    150

Adding favourite artists to Last.fm manually         152

Listening to music on Last.fm                        154

Seeing recommended music on Last.fm                  155

Introduction to Blip.fm                              157

Signing up for Blip.fm                               158

Searching for a song on Blip.fm                      159

Blipping a song                                      160

Introduction to Spotify                              161

Getting a Spotify account                            162

Installing Spotify                                   163

Importing your music to Spotify                      164

Playing a song on Spotify                            165

Seeing an artist's playlist                          166

Seeing all songs on an album                         167

Starring songs                                       168

Creating and sharing playlists on Spotify            169

Finding Facebook friends on Spotify                  171

# Introduction

When it comes to music, people not only love to share what bands they like, they also like to learn what their friends are listening to. Discovering new music can, in a way, be as enjoyable as listening to old favourites.

In this chapter, I'll cover a few services that offer social music possibilities (Last.fm, Blip.fm and Spotify). With any luck, one of them will be your favourite source for discovering new music.

# Introduction to Last.fm

Need new music? Then Last.fm is your best bet. It uses an algorithm that 'scrobbles' your current music collection and then suggests other music that you might also like. So far, there are over 50 billion scrobbles in the service.

The service is free and can analyse music files on your hard drive or on other music services like Spotify.

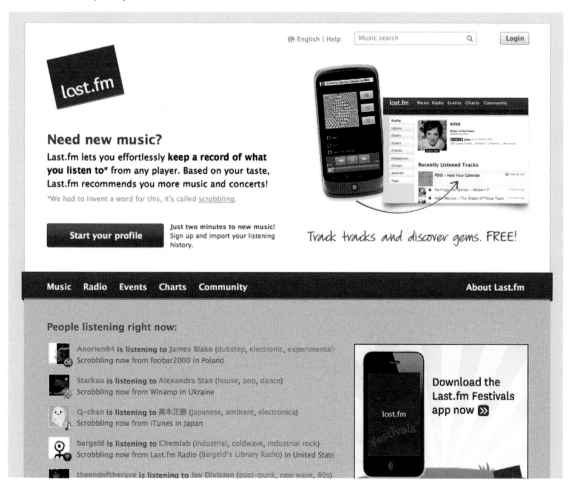

# Starting a Last.fm profile

To get started with Last.fm:

**1** Point your browser to www.last.fm.

**2** Click Start your profile.

**3** On the registration form, you can connect with Facebook, or register by entering a username, email address, password and other information.

Already have an account? Log in

**Join Last.fm**

We'll help you find new music

last.fm

**f** Connect with Facebook (optional)   **3**

**Choose your username**

Maximum 15 characters, no spaces please.

**Type your email address**

**Choose a password**

**Type the words below**

X-total etungern

Powered by reCAPTCHA

☐ I agree to the Terms of Use and Privacy Policy and confirm that I am 13 years of age or over.

Create my profile

# Get music recommendations from Last.fm

Once you're set up with Last.fm, you'll be directed to a dashboard page. To start getting music recommendations, you can

- Enter a list of your favourite artists, separated with commas

OR

- Download the Scrobbler software to analyse your music library.

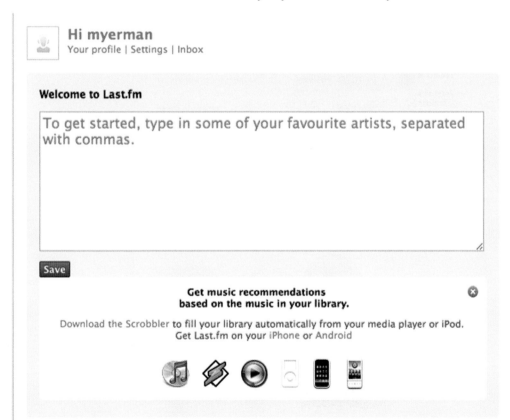

# Downloading the Last.fm Scrobbler

If you're anything like me, you have a fairly large collection of music, and typing in the names of favourite artists one by one wouldn't just be tedious, you'd miss quite a few. So the best thing to do is click the appropriate icon for the music player you have and download the Scrobbler.

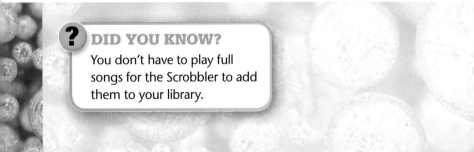

1. As soon as you register with Last.fm, start listening to music with your music player (in my case, I'm using iTunes).

2. As you listen to music, you'll notice that artists are added to your Music Library on Last.fm.

# Adding favourite artists to Last.fm manually

You can always add your own artists manually to the library. Below, you can see that I've added half a dozen favourites. When I hit save, Last.fm adds these artists to my library.

**Hi myerman**
Your profile | Settings | Inbox

**Welcome to Last.fm**

Sting, Royal Crown Revue, Salsa Celtica, Jimi Hendrix, Duke Ellington, Creedence Clearwater Revival

Save

**myerman's Library**                                        ⚙ Settings

Thanks! We've started your music profile by adding the 6 artists you typed to your Library. Continue building your profile by listening to music, or with the [ + Add to Library ] buttons on music pages.

**6 Artists in total**
Showing: Overall

To see any individual artist, I click on their icon. Below is the Last.fm page for Salsa Celtica, one of my favourite bands (they combine Salsa and Celtic sounds, check them out).

Notice that I can visit other, similar artists by clicking on their profiles. I can also view more details about this particular band by clicking on the tabs on the left.

Artist

Biography

Pictures

Videos

Albums

Tracks

Events

News

Charts

Similar Artists

Tags

Listeners

Journal

Groups

## Salsa Celtica ON TOUR

**90,397 plays (13,109 listeners)**
0 plays in your library

Shop now at Amazon | Send Salsa Celtica Ringtones to Cell

More options ▾    Tag

Salsa Celtica – an 11 piece world music fusion band coming from Edinburgh, Scotland, formed in 1995. They have released four studio albums so far.

Edit

See all 2 pictures

▶ Play Salsa Celtica Radio

**Popular tags:** salsa, celtic, latin, folk, scottish  See more | Tag this
**Shouts:** 14 shouts

**Share this artist:**

✉ Send    Tweet    +1

Recommend  1    Send

## Similar Artists

| Mamborama | Sonora Carruseles | Africando | Los Van Van | Orquesta de la Luz | Peatbog Faeries | Fruko y Sus Tesos |

See more

# Listening to music on Last.fm

Once you're on an artist's profile page, you can start listening to music by clicking on Play [artist name] Radio, where [artist name] is the name of your artist.

## Salsa Celtica ON TOUR

90,397 plays (13,109 listeners)
0 plays in your library

Shop now at Amazon | Send Salsa Celtica Ringtones to Cell

More options ▼    Tag

Salsa Celtica – an 11 piece world music fusion band coming from Edinburgh, Scotland, formed in 1995. They have released four studio albums so far.

See all 2 pictures ➲

▶ Play Salsa Celtica Radio

As soon as you do that, Last.fm will load a music player that will start playing songs by your artist. You can share tracks with your friends on Twitter or Facebook, you can add tags to the tracks to make them easy to find, and you can buy the tracks on iTunes and other online retailers.

# Seeing recommended music on Last.fm

Once you've got some artists loaded into Last.fm, the service will start recommending music to you. To see your music recommendations, simply go back to the Last.fm home page.

You'll see a list of artists with a link to view the complete list of recommendations.

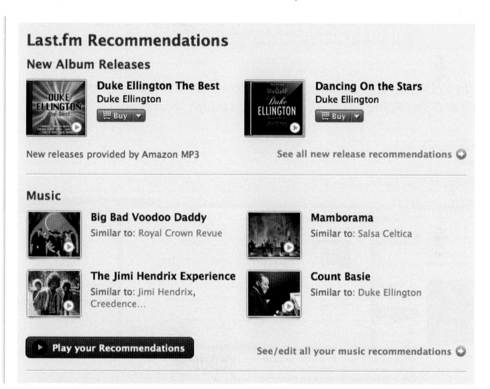

Once you click through to the complete list, you can filter your recommendations down by genre. On the next page I've filtered the list by 'classic rock' and see that one of my favourite bands, The Police, is on the list.

I click Add to Library and get a pop-up window that asks me to confirm this action. I click Save and The Police are now part of my Last.fm library.

# Introduction to Blip.fm

Ever wanted to be a DJ, entertaining people with your musical selections? Think you've got really great taste in music and want to share that taste with other people? Then you need to check out Blip.fm.

With Blip.fm, you sign up as a 'DJ' and can then stream free music on a radio station that others can subscribe to. It's a fun way to discover and share music with your friends.

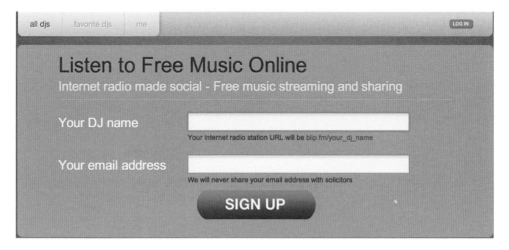

# Signing up for Blip.fm

Signing up for Blip.fm is relatively painless:

**1** Point your browser at www.blip.fm.

**2** Register a unique DJ name (for example, mine is myerman).

**3** Enter an email address.

**4** Click Sign Up.

**5** Once you're logged in, you should see a dashboard.

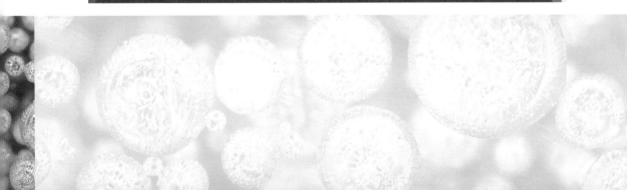

# Searching for a song on Blip.fm

Before you can do anything else on Blip.fm, you have to be able to find a song and then play it.

To search for a song on Blip.fm, follow these steps:

1. Make sure you're logged into Blip.fm.

2. Type the name of an artist or song in the search field and click Search.

3. Blip.fm will return a list of songs that match your search criteria. As you can see, I did a search for Led Zeppelin. The songs in this list are usually hosted on YouTube, and can range from videos of live performances by the original band to covers of that song by another band, or (more recently) people playing a tribute to that song on their own instruments.

4. When you find an appropriate version of the song, you can click Preview to listen in.

# Blipping a song

Once you've searched for a song, previewed it and found it to your liking, you're ready to play the song, or 'blip' it.

To 'blip' a song:

**1** Make sure you're logged into Blip.fm.

**2** Do a search for a song or artist as described in the previous section.

**3** Click Blip next to the song.

**4** You can add a message to the song.

**5** You can also share your 'blip' with other networks, like Twitter and Facebook.

**6** Click Blip.

| all djs | favorite djs | me | find djs · invite friends | blog · sessions |

**What artist / song do you want to Blip?** **3**

Led Zeppelin – Kashmir ✕

Add a message 150

**4**

Send Blips to Other Websites ▾

**5** Toggle / Add: 

**6** BLIP

**?** **DID YOU KNOW?**

Blip.fm will add a link to your 'blip' so that other users can listen to the song on Blip.fm directly.

# Introduction to Spotify

Spotify bills itself as a new way of listening to music. When you create an account and download the Spotify application, it will import the music files already on your hard drive, then allow you to share music playlists with your friends. You can also synch your playlists with other computers and even mobile devices.

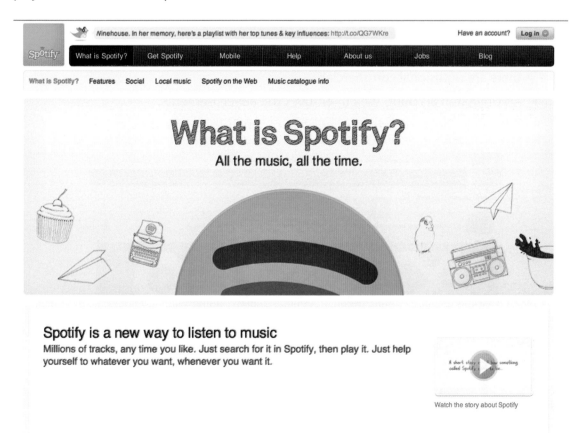

# Getting a Spotify account

To sign up for a Spotify account:

**1** Point your browser at www.spotify.com.

**2** Click Get Spotify on the navigation bar.

**3** You have three choices when you sign up:

- A free account, which allows you to play local files and share with friends, but there are occasional commercials.
- An Unlimited account, which removes the advertisements.
- A Premium account, which allows you to synch to mobile devices.

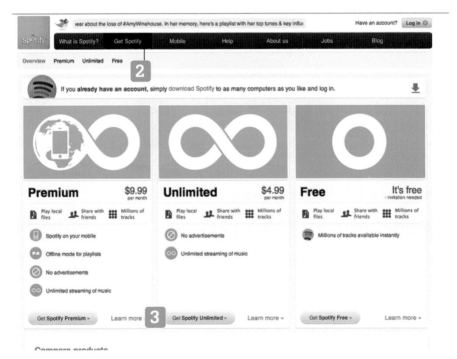

# Installing Spotify

Once you've set up an account with Spotify, you can download the Spotify player. Once it's downloaded and installed, you will see a screen similar to this one:

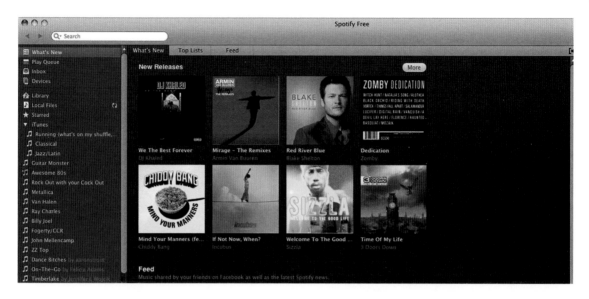

# Importing your music to Spotify

Once you've got Spotify up and running, click Local Files in the left-hand navigation pane to start importing music from your local music player.

After a few minutes, your music library on Spotify will start to fill in and will look something like this:

# Playing a song on Spotify

To play a song on Spotify, simply double-click the name of the song or track in the list.

The Spotify footer will contain the controls you need to pause, rewind and fast forward the song. You'll also see controls for adjusting the volume.

# Seeing an artist's playlist

To find out more about the artist playing a song, all you have to do is click the name of the artist. You can find this name in the Artist column, usually to the right of the song or track.

Below, I've clicked the link for the artist a-ha, that wonderful one-hit wonder from the 1980s. As you can see, Spotify provides you with a short bio, a list of top hits and available albums.

You can play any of the songs on this list, even if you don't own that particular song. You can also right-click a track and add any song to a playlist, for example.

# Seeing all songs on an album

Just as you can discover all music by an artist, you might want to find all songs on an album. You can do this by clicking the name of the album in the Album column.

Below, I've clicked the album *The Very Best of Bananarama* (continuing the 1980s theme).

# Starring songs

When you 'star' a song on Spotify, you're indicating that it's a favourite. You can star any song, whether it's in your local playlist or not, by clicking the star icon to the left of the track name.

| | | Track | Artist | Time | Album | |
|---|---|---|---|---|---|---|
| | ↪ | Pressure | Billy Joel | 4:37 | Greatest Hits, Vol. II (19... | ♪ |
| ★ | ↪ | When The Going Gets Tough, The Tou... | Billy Ocean | 4:09 | **Billy Ocean: Greatest Hits** | ♪ |
| | ↪ | Caribbean Queen (No More Love On T... | Billy Ocean | 4:07 | Billy Ocean: Greatest Hits | ♪ |
| | ↪ | Loverboy | Billy Ocean | 4:10 | Billy Ocean: Greatest Hits | ♪ |
| | ↪ | Get Outta My Dreams, Get Into My Car | Billy Ocean | 4:45 | Billy Ocean: Greatest Hits | ♪ |
| | ↪ | No Rain | Blind Melon | 3:37 | Blind Melon | ♪ |
| | ↪ | Old Time Rock & Roll | Bob Seger | 3:14 | Greatest Hits | ♪ |
| | ↪ | Rockin Robin | Bobby Day | 2:37 | Warwick-Doo Wop Groups | ♪ |
| | ↪ | Lay Your Hands On Me | Bon Jovi | 5:59 | Cross Road | ♪ |

All the songs you've starred show up in the Starred section of Spotify, which you can access by clicking on Starred in the left navigation pane.

★ **Starred**   9 tracks,

This is a list of music that you have starred

| | | Track | Artist | Time | Album | | Added |
|---|---|---|---|---|---|---|---|
| ★ | ↪ | The Distance | Cake | 3:00 | Fashion Nugget | ♪ | a moment ago |
| ★ | ↪ | Mandolin Rain - Remastered 2003 | Bruce Hornsby | 5:18 | Bruce Hornsby: Greatest... | ♪ | a moment ago |
| ★ | ↪ | The Way It Is | Bruce Hornsby | 4:57 | The Way It Is | ♪ | a moment ago |
| ★ | ↪ | Short Skirt/Long Jacket | Cake | 3:24 | Comfort Eagle | ♪ | a moment ago |
| ★ | ↪ | Rock Around the Clock | Bill Haley & His Comets | 2:12 | Rock Around the Clock | ♪ | a moment ago |
| ★ | ↪ | Fight For Your Right | The Beastie Boys | 3:27 | Licensed To III | ♪ | a moment ago |
| ★ | ↪ | In Your Room | The Bangles | 3:30 | The Essential Bangles | ♪ | a moment ago |
| ★ | ↪ | What's Up? | 4 Non Blondes | 4:55 | Bigger, Better, Faster, More ! | ♪ | a moment ago |
| ★ | ↪ | Kryptonite | 3 Doors Down | 3:54 | The Better Life | ♪ | a moment ago |

# Creating and sharing playlists on Spotify

Now that Spotify knows about your music tastes, it's time to create a playlist and publish it. A playlist is just a group of songs, and it's up to you to set the criteria. Have a favourite artist? Create a top 10 playlist for that artist. Or maybe you want to feature songs with heavy blues guitar. Or songs by female singers that hit the top of the charts in 1993. It doesn't matter, you can create any kind of list you like.

To add songs to a playlist:

**1** Right-click the song you want to add to a playlist.

**2** On the pop-up window, select Add To.

**3** If you want to add the song to an existing playlist, choose it from the list. Otherwise, choose New Playlist.

**4** As you add songs to a playlist, it'll appear in the left navigation pane. You can then click the name of the playlist to see the songs in that playlist.

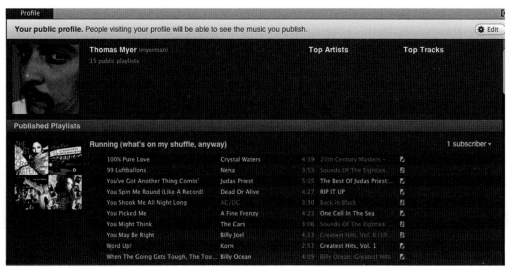

To publish a playlist:

- Right-click the list you want to publish.
- Make sure that Publish is ticked.

Now, when friends visit your profile, they will see your published playlists.

# Finding Facebook friends on Spotify

You've uploaded your music, created and published playlists and now it's time to invite your Facebook friends to the party.

To find your Facebook friends:

**1** On the File menu, choose Connect to Facebook.

**2** When prompted, log on to Facebook.

**3** When prompted, decide whether you want to send a note to your Facebook friends that you are on Spotify. Everyone in your Facebook stream will see it, including those who aren't on Spotify.

**4** As soon as you've successfully connected to Facebook, you'll see a list of Facebook friends with Spotify accounts appear on the right. You can click any of these friends to see their profile and start exploring their playlists.

**5** You can even subscribe to any playlist by clicking Subscribe next to any playlist.

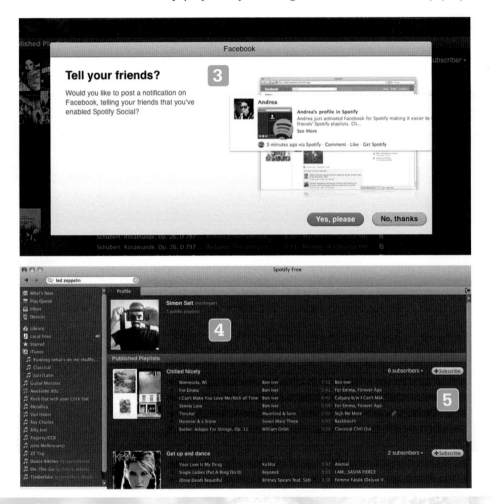

# 9 Location-based services

| | |
|---|---|
| Downloading Gowalla | 175 |
| Checking in to a location | 176 |
| About Me in Gowalla | 177 |
| Finding friends on Gowalla | 178 |
| Introduction to Foursquare | 179 |
| Downloading the app | 180 |
| Checking in to a location | 181 |
| Using Foursquare to explore | 182 |
| Using Facebook check-ins | 183 |
| Using Google+ check-ins | 184 |

# Introduction

If you've got a smartphone, such as an iPhone or Android, love to visit and discover new coffee shops, museums, nightclubs and other locations, and you're on social media, well, the next logical step is to sign up for a location-based service.

What's a location-based service? Technically speaking, it's any service that lets you 'check in' to a place you're visiting and then share your presence with friends on a social network like Twitter or Facebook.

Some location-based services, like Gowalla and Foursquare, offer their own independent apps that let you check in to places; other services, like Facebook and Google+, have added check-ins as part of their service.

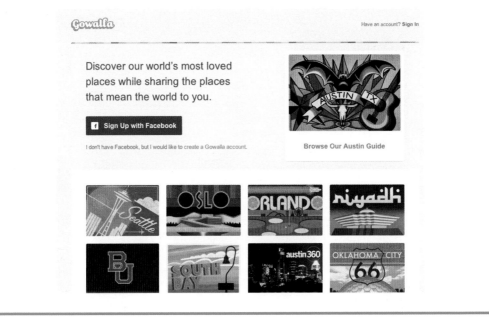

# Downloading Gowalla

Gowalla is a social location game, available on iPhone, Android and BlackBerry. To download it to your phone:

**1** Log on to the App Store that's right for your phone.

**2** Search for Gowalla.

**3** Tap the icon to install.

**4** Once you've downloaded and installed it, tap the icon to open the application.

**5** If you haven't joined yet, either register for the first time by entering your email address or use Facebook to join.

**6** Once you've logged in, you will see a Gowalla welcome screen. Tap that to see the home screen.

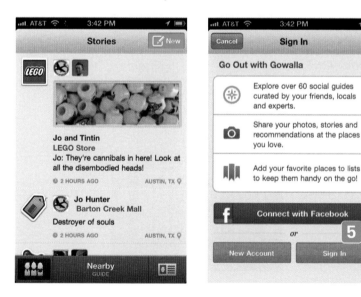

**WHAT DOES THIS MEAN?**

**Check in:** When you check in to a location in Gowalla, you get a stamp on your passport. It's like a record of you having visited that place.

# Checking in to a location

Now that you have Gowalla on your smartphone, the next time you're out and about, give it a try. If you're at a nightclub or museum and you'd like people to know where you are, follow these steps:

**1** Open the Gowalla application on your phone.

**2** Tap the New button (it's green and white in the upper right corner). This will create a new Check In, or as it's referred to in Gowalla, a new 'story'.

**3** Pick a spot from the list of spots Gowalla shows you, or add one of your own.

**4** List the people you're with and then click Done.

**5** Once you've 'checked in' you can add photos and comments.

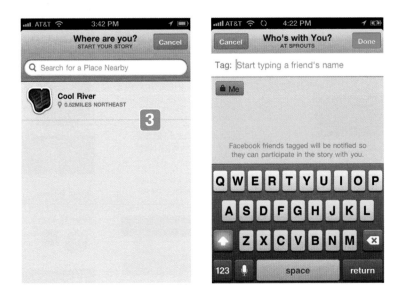

**ALERT:** There may or may not be privacy considerations at play with location-based services. You don't have to share a check in on Facebook or Twitter if you don't want to!

# About Me in Gowalla

In Gowalla, you can control your profile by visiting the About Me page. It contains a record of all the stamps and pins you've collected, lists all the people you follow and who follow you.

To view your About Me page:

**1** Tap the rolodex card icon in the lower right.

**2** Tap the About <your name> button.

**3** You can view your stamps and pins by tapping the appropriate buttons.

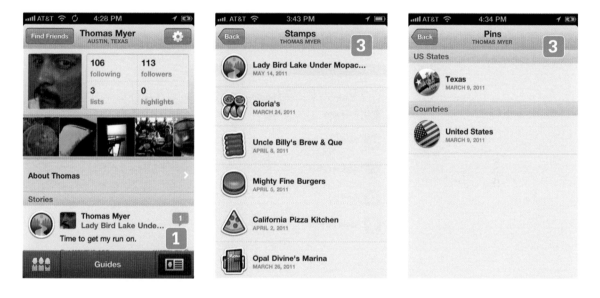

## WHAT DOES THIS MEAN?

**Pins:** You can collect pins by completing challenges and trips. A challenge in Gowalla might be something simple, like visit the same bar three times in a single week. Or visiting all the museums in a single city.

# Finding friends on Gowalla

What's the point of being on Gowalla if you aren't connecting with friends? Well, there isn't much point, and this is all about social location, right?

To find friends on Gowalla:

**1** In the Gowalla app, tap the rolodex card icon in the lower right corner then tap the Find Friends button.

**2** You'll see a menu that provides a list of options for finding friends. Currently you can import friends from Facebook, Twitter, Gmail, your own address book, or by inviting people via SMS.

**3** Tap one of the service options. Below you can see I've tapped Twitter. A list of my Twitter friends appears and I can add them one at a time or tap Add All.

# Introduction to Foursquare

The other major player in the social location game is Foursquare. Foursquare is slightly different from Gowalla in that it is more competitive. The goal of Foursquare is to become 'mayor' of different locations. The only way to become 'mayor' is to check in as many times as you can.

If you have a favourite pub or other location that's close to you, then checking in a number of times will be quite easy and will earn you mayorships. If you only check in occasionally, or are on holiday and will probably never visit a location again, you can go ahead and check in, but it's likely you'll never become mayor.

Along the way, you can also earn points and virtual badges. With over 10 million users and over 3 million check-ins every day, Foursquare is certainly a busy place.

# Downloading the app

If you're on an iPhone, Android, Palm device or BlackBerry, you can download
Foursquare and start checking in to places.

**1** Log on to the App Store that's right for your phone.

**2** Search for Foursquare.

**3** Tap the icon to install.

**4** After the application downloads and installs to your phone, tap the icon to start the
app.

**5** You'll be prompted to either register with your email address or use Facebook.

**6** As soon as you register, Foursquare will prompt you to add friends. If you've
registered using your Facebook account, you'll see a list of your Facebook friends.

**7** You can add friends by tapping the + sign next to their names.

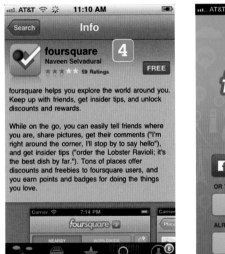

# Checking in to a location

Once you have the Foursquare application installed on your phone, the next time you're at your favourite location, it's time to check in!

To check in on Foursquare:

**1** Open the Foursquare app on your phone.

**2** Tap Check In (it's in the footer navigation).

**3** Foursquare will show you a list of nearby locations. Tap the entry matching your location.

**4** On the next screen, tap Check In Here to check in.

# Using Foursquare to explore

One of the more fun things about participating in social location games like Foursquare is the ability to see where other people have been recently. Whether you're visiting a new city or if you're just looking for a new coffeehouse, bar, nightclub or hangout in your home town, you can explore options right on your smartphone.

To explore:

**1** Open the Foursquare app on your phone.

**2** Tap Explore (it's in the footer navigation to the left of Check In).

**3** If you want, you can limit your explorations to a certain category (such as food) and then drill down further into types of food (pizza, sandwiches and so on).

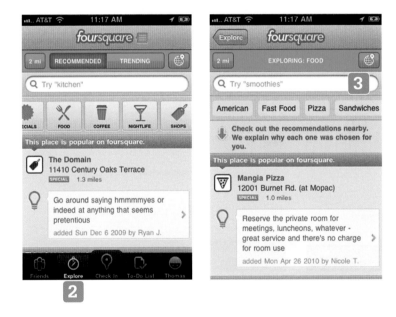

# Using Facebook check-ins

You don't have to be a member of Gowalla or Foursquare to participate in the social location fun. If you're a Facebook member and are using the Facebook smartphone app, you can also check in to your favourite places.

To check in on Facebook:

**1** Open the Facebook app.

**2** Tap Check In when you're at your location. The Check In button is in the top right corner, next to Status.

**3** Facebook will show you a list of nearby locations. Either tap the one that's appropriate, or do a search for the right location.

**4** On the final screen, add a note to your check-in, tag anyone who is also there with you and tap Check In.

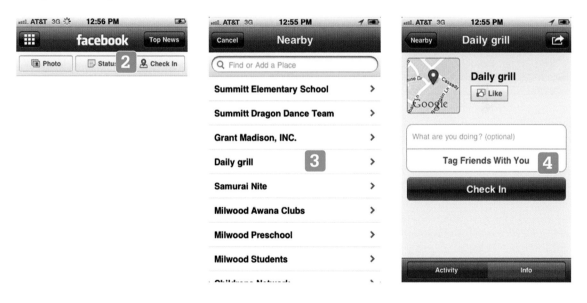

**ALERT:** Some people may view you including them in a check-in as a violation of their privacy. It's always wise to ask permission before you check someone in.

# Using Google+ check-ins

The new Google+ social network's mobile application (available on Android and iPhone at the time of writing) also allows you to check in to places.

To check in using Google+:

1 Open the Google+ app on your phone.

2 When you're at your location, tap the check-in button. It looks like a tickbox in the upper right corner.

3 Google+ will show you a list of nearby venues. Either tap the one that matches your location, or do a search to find the right one.

4 On the next screen, add a note and choose which circle you want to share your check-in with. You can also add a photo.

5 Click Post when you've finished.

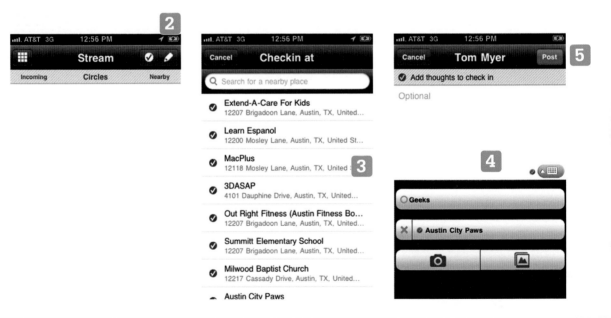

# 10 Fun social websites to try out

DailyBooth                                    187

Delicious                                     188

Flixster                                      189

Friends Reunited                              190

GoodReads                                     191

The Hotlist                                   192

TravBuddy                                     193

Yelp                                          194

DailyMile                                     195

Ravelry                                       196

# Introduction

The world of social media isn't just limited to the big popular services like Facebook, Twitter, YouTube and Google+ of course. There are lots of other, more specialised services out there that allow people to connect around their specific passions, like good books or fitness.

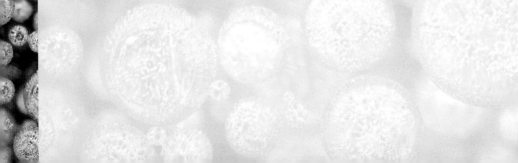

# DailyBooth

DailyBooth is a fun little site that allows people to upload a picture of themselves every day. It bills itself as a community site where you communicate with your daily picture – after a few weeks on the site, it's interesting to see the kinds of stories people tell with pictures!

Site: DailyBooth.com

# Delicious

Delicious is an online bookmarking service that liberates your bookmarks from your browser. We've all experienced the frustration of not being at the computer we need to access a bookmark. So instead of bookmarking sites on your own computer, do it on Delicious and then share what you've discovered with others. Makes for a fantastic research tool.

Site: Delicious.com

# Flixster

If you love films, then you'll love being a member of Flixster. Members review and rate films, interact with each other about films, share news and gossip, and more. With Flixster, you can also find out when films are opening and when DVDs will be available.

Site: Flixster.com

**Brave**
Pixar's latest!

**Mission: Impossible**
Ghost Protocol!

**War Horse**
Steven Spielberg is back!

**30 Minutes or Less**
Hotter than pizza.

**Brave**
Pixar gets *Brave!* See the trailer now!

| Top Box Office | Opening | New DVDs |
| --- | --- | --- |

1

**Harry Potter and the Deathly Hallows - Part 2**
🍺 **93% liked it**
Daniel Radcliffe, Rupert Grint, Emma Watson, Helena Bonham Carter
PG-13, 2 hr. 10 min.

# Friends Reunited

Friends Reunited was the first popular social networking site in the United Kingdom and is still going strong. Founded in 1999, the site's mission is to help you reunite with old school friends, former colleagues and even long-lost relatives. It uses a unique system of double-blind email addresses that allows complete privacy on both ends of a conversation.

Site: FriendsReunited.com

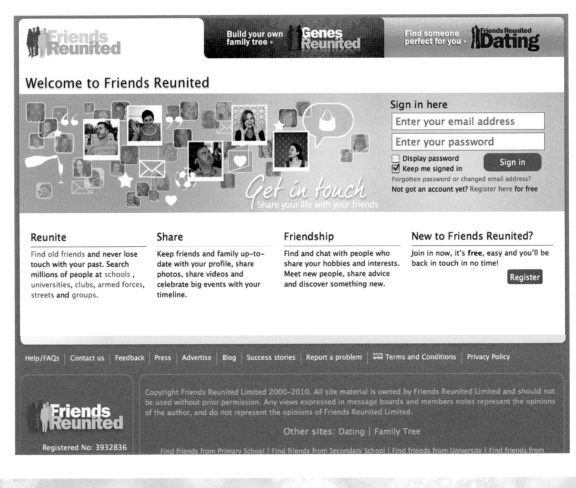

# GoodReads

If you love books and reading, and love to interact with others who also love books, then you definitely need to check out GoodReads. When you first log on, you're asked to review some books you've read. As soon as you've rated them, you're given recommendations on other books and can connect with friends on Twitter and Facebook.

Site: GoodReads.com

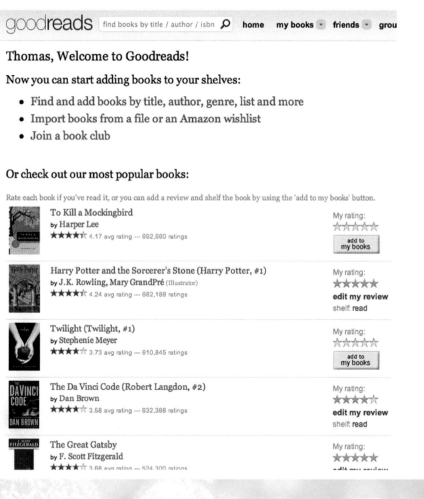

# The Hotlist

The Hotlist is a private social network that helps you and your friends coordinate an evening out. You can follow what your Facebook friends are doing for an evening out and use the Coordinate feature to coordinate a night out on the town.

Site: Hotlist.com

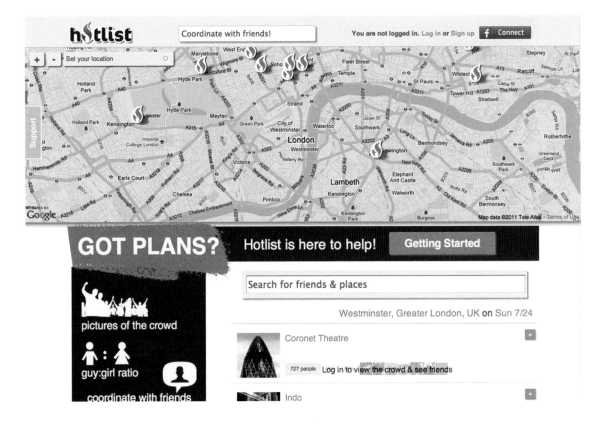

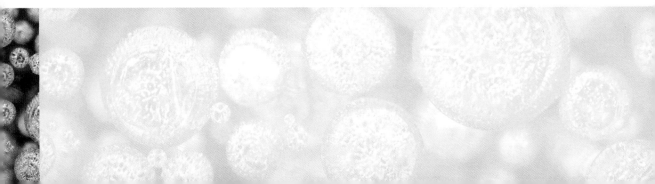

# TravBuddy

TravBuddy is a social network for travellers. You can research your future travels, meet and connect with other travellers and share travel advice. The main focus of the site is to connect you with an experienced traveller who is also going to your destination.

Site: TravBuddy.com

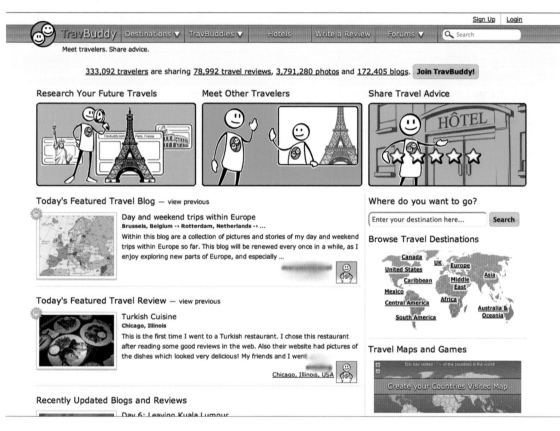

# Yelp

Yelp is a site devoted to allowing people write reviews of local businesses. If you're visiting a new city and aren't sure about the quality of the food at a certain restaurant, do a search for that business on Yelp to see if it has any reviews. Most of the time, you'll find the reviews helpful.

Site: Yelp.com

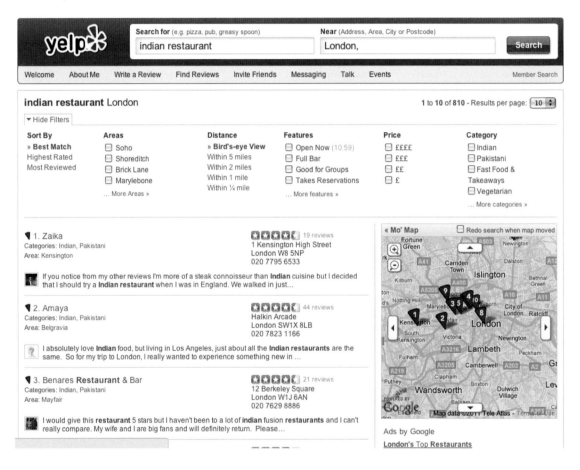

# DailyMile

If you're a runner, cyclist or other distance athlete, then you really need to check out DailyMile. You can register with your Facebook account and then start tracking your workouts using a smartphone application. This information gets shared with your friends, who can help keep you motivated!

Site: DailyMile.com

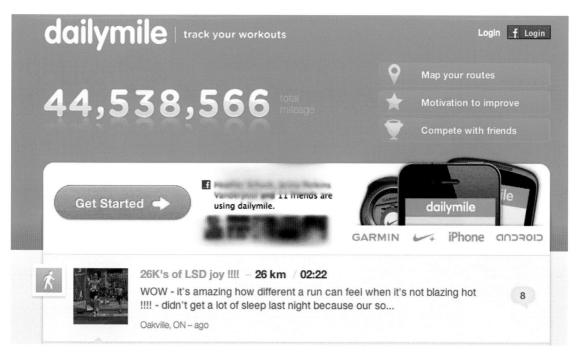

# Ravelry

Ravelry is a social network for knitters, crocheters and other 'crafty' people. If you're the kind of person who makes their own sweaters, scarves, hats and mittens, then Ravelry will become your new home away from home. Members post photos of their ongoing projects, give each other advice on different aspects of crafting and have lots of chances to connect and interact.

Site: Ravelry.com

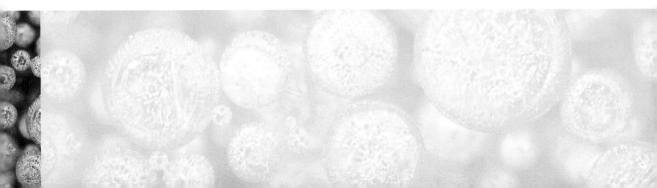

# Top 10 Social Networking Problems Solved

| | | |
|---|---|---|
| 1 | Privacy issues | 198 |
| 2 | Security issues | 199 |
| 3 | Oversharing | 201 |
| 4 | Inauthenticity | 202 |
| 5 | Friending too many people | 204 |
| 6 | Friending too few people | 206 |
| 7 | Trolls | 208 |
| 8 | Forgetting the social part of social media | 209 |
| 9 | Getting distracted by too much social media | 211 |
| 10 | Not participating enough in social media | 213 |

# Problem 1: Privacy issues

The biggest concern that many people have regarding social media is that of privacy. After all, if you're actively telling people what you are doing, where you are and what you are thinking, then privacy can be a very big problem. I've known people who had to stop using certain services (like location-based services) because they felt that too many people knew exactly where they were going to be and would 'run into them' by chance there.

Some people think that being on social media means you have to give up privacy altogether. Not true at all. Most of the major services, like Twitter and Facebook, allow you to create some privacy for yourself. On Twitter, for example, you can make your account protected, so that people can follow you only after you approve them. On Facebook, you can decide whether only your friends can see what you're posting.

With all social networks, the best way to ensure privacy is to:

1. Have good control over who is your friend on any given network.

2. Only divulge very personal information on certain networks where you keep your friends very close. Many people use Facebook for this purpose and then use Twitter or other services to publish other information.

**SEE ALSO:** If you're really concerned about your Facebook privacy, check out http://www.reclaimprivacy.org/. You can scan your Facebook profile to see how private it is.

# Problem 2: Security issues

All social media services exist on the Internet and that means they are vulnerable to hacking attempts and other nefarious activity by either mischievous or malicious persons. Don't believe any of the hype – if a web site is online, at some point, someone will try to hack into it.

## MakePassword

One of the easiest **online password generators** which can generate a single random password or lists of hundreds of random passwords. You choose the character sets, password length and the quantity to create. Hash values can also be created for your convenience. This password generator is useful for getting a random password for personal use or for generating large lists of default passwords.

Password Length: 8    (4 - 64 chars)
Quantity: 1    (2500 max)

○Characters to Use

☑ Lower Case Characters (e.g. abcdef)
☑ Upper Case Characters (e.g. ABCDEF)
☐ Numbers (e.g. 012345)
☐ Symbols (e.g. /!@#$%^*()_+=-')

○Create type-safe passwords

☑ Exclude l, i, I, 0, O, o, 1

○Provide hash values

☐ SHA1 ☐ MD5
☐ Include Random Salt (added to hash)

○Password Strength

☐ Include Password Strength (0 to 100)

○How to present results

⦿ Webpage ○ CSV File ○ Plain Text File

( Make Password(s) )

▶ **SEE ALSO:** Running out of ideas for new passwords? Check out http://maord.com/. It will help you generate hundreds of secure, random passwords.

Here's how you can improve your online security:

1. Use very strong passwords – at least eight characters in length, use upper and lower letters, at least one or two digits, and at least one or two special characters (like !, % or # if possible).

2. Use a different password for different services. If that's too complicated, you might try different variations on the password that include an abbreviation of the service you're on.

   For example, your basic password might be p4SSw0rd!. On Facebook, that password might be FB_p4SSw0rd!, and on Twitter it might be T_p4SSw0rd!. All you have to remember is what service it's on and you're set.

3. Another thing to consider is that many social media services give you the option of using your Facebook or Twitter credentials to log in. You should use these systems as often as possible as they keep you more secure – in all cases these systems use anonymous tokens that don't contain any information about you specifically, just that you are a member in good standing with Facebook or Twitter.

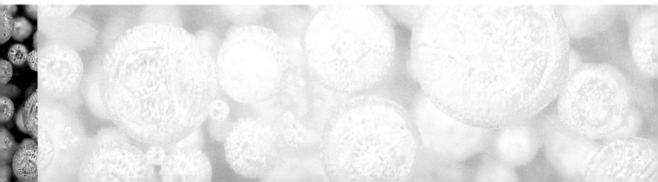

# Problem 3: Oversharing

One of the biggest perils of social media and social networks in general is a problem called oversharing. We're all prone to do it. We get angry, or sad, or something really bothers us, and we end up going on a rant – divulging information about a bad relationship, a lousy work situation, a horrible boss, a love affair gone bad, or vent our frustrations or even maybe suicidal thoughts.

I've seen people get fired or reprimanded at their jobs for oversharing on Twitter. I myself have lost various business opportunities by speaking frankly about my anti-religious feelings. In the long run, I've earned the respect and friendship of many others, but it's probably not such a good idea to let everything hang out, if you will.

Oversharing isn't just limited to what you say. Pictures of you doing stupid or crazy things (while inebriated, for example) will eventually be seen by many more people than you think. The same goes for videos of you at a party or maybe saying things you thought were being said in private.

If you don't want to see it on the front page of your local newspaper, then it's best not to put it on social media.

Here are a few tips to keep you from oversharing:

1. If you don't want your spouse or mother (or grandmother) to see it, then don't put it on a social network.

2. If you're very angry with someone, then it's best to walk away from the computer or turn off the smartphone.

3. If you think your boss might fire you for posting a photograph or saying something on Twitter or Facebook, then you'd better keep it to yourself.

 **DID YOU KNOW?**

There are many web sites devoted to funny (and very sad) oversharing Facebook incidents. Just google 'Facebook overshare' or go to http://failbook.failblog.org for a sample.

# Problem 4: Inauthenticity

Another big problem with social media is inauthenticity. A lot of people might overshare and therefore reveal their 'true' selves, but many others have online personas that are nothing like their real selves. They use their Twitter and Facebook accounts to send out endless solicitations for some product or never answer replies or engage in conversation.

Remember, social media isn't magic – it's just another opportunity to get to know other people. Nobody's perfect, far from it, but also, nobody is a 24/7 endless bore with nothing interesting to share.

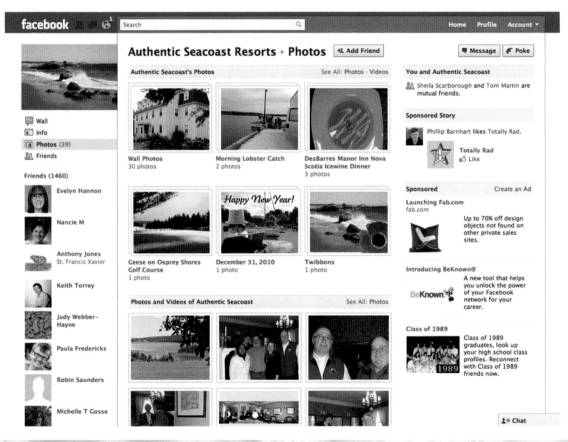

If you're into photography, or travelling, or knitting, or gardening, then for goodness sake, be authentic and tell your friends what you're up to! You'll be surprised how much they'll enjoy your contributions.

But how do you share 'authentic' information?

1. What kinds of hobbies give you pleasure? In other words, what are the things you like to do regardless of being paid for them? These are authentic things to talk about.

2. What kinds of reactions do you have when you experience new things, such as travelling to a distant country? Do you experience awe or wonder when seeing artwork in a museum or incredible mountains? Please share!

3. Have you just had a very positive interaction with friends, family or strangers? Having a good time on holiday? Seeing a long-lost relative for the first time in a long time? These are great things to post on social media.

# Problem 5: Friending too many people

Some people use services like Facebook and Twitter to befriend a whole bunch of people. You'll look at their profile pages and they've got 3,000 Facebook friends and follow 5,000 people on Twitter. Now, there are quite a few people I know who travel for business and come into contact with lots of people, and they actually do want to keep in contact with them, but you will know when too many is too many.

There are any number of studies out there that reference a Dunbar number (named after a noted anthropologist). This number represents the maximum number of meaningful relationships a person can have at any given time. That number is usually around 150, give or take a few depending on your circumstances. In other words, when I see someone with 5,000 Facebook friends, I always wonder which 150 of those people are the nearest and dearest to that person's heart.

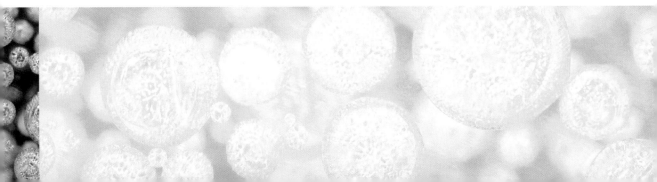

Don't get me wrong, it's a free country and you can do what you like, but you'll find that friending that many people will lead you to miss out on the important things posted by friends and family.

Now, you'll notice that I follow about 2,000 people on Twitter. You're probably thinking to yourself, 'Aha, what's good for the goose isn't good for the gander!' Well, I also use Twitter groups and follow those more avidly than I do my main Twitter timeline. For example, I've put about 100 people in a 'Buddies' list (it includes my wife @hopedoty) and that's where I put most of my attention when I'm on Twitter. I have other lists for political friends, comedians, breaking news and so forth, and each of those gets a column in Tweetdeck. It helps me cope with everything that's happening out there and still maintain lots of loose connections with people.

▶ **SEE ALSO:** For more information on creating and using Twitter lists, check out http://support.twitter.com/entries/76460-how-to-use-twitter-lists.

# Problem 6: Friending too few people

The opposite problem to friending too many people is friending only a few people. You visit someone's Twitter or Facebook profile and they have 10 friends. In my experience you have to get up to around a few dozen people on a social network before you can start having interesting conversations.

Take a chance – explore a bit, reach out and connect with people, especially when you meet them at a social event in real life. You'll find that your enjoyment of social media will go up a great deal.

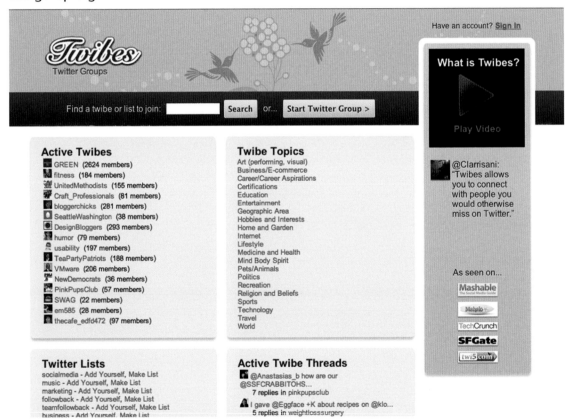

Here in Austin, Texas (where I live) there is a very tight and talkative group of about 1,000 people (most of whom follow each other on Twitter and other services like Facebook) and we keep tabs on each other. It's like living in a city within a city. We laugh together, keep tabs on each other and have a lot of fun.

An easy way to find more friends on social media:

1. Do a Google search for your favourite hobby or pastime.

2. Focus on any Facebook pages, blogs and Twitter users who come up in the search results.

3. Visit these blogs, Facebook pages and Twitter profiles and see if you can strike up an online conversation – leave a comment, say hello, like that.

4. See if there's anything happening in your local region. For example, you may notice that this person who avidly collects stamps is active in a local stamp collectors' group, or that he or she is organising a cruise or outing that allows stamp collectors to socialise and have fun. By all means, find out when the next meeting is and get to know people!

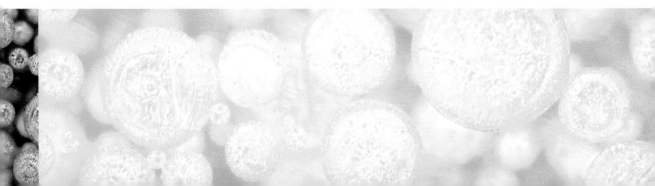

# Problem 7: Trolls

Trolls, to the uninitiated, are those people who act rudely online just to get everyone's blood up. They may be paid to do this, by either a PR firm or a political action group, or they may just enjoy the feeling of getting everyone into a big online brawl.

For example, you might write a great blog post about how you and a group of colleagues (all of you being women) have made great contributions as women to a particular industry or in your local business district. A troll might show up to add a comment to your blog that in effect casts doubts on any woman being smart enough to be in business. Before you know it, there is a screaming fistfight happening on your blog, with everyone slinging mud back and forth, and you find that all those good feelings you had about your achievement have evaporated.

Trolls have always existed on the Internet, and they always will exist. The best thing to do with a troll is to ignore him (trolls almost always are un- or under-employed males in their early twenties) and just keep on doing your thing. It's only when you give attention to a troll that they grow in power.

How to deal with trolls:

**1** The best way is to ignore them. Trolls feed on your attention. Don't respond to them and they will go away.

**2** If you can't ignore them, or if they get abusive, then try to report them to the blog owner (for example). Perhaps they can be banned or blocked.

**3** Trolls will probably own multiple accounts on any one site, and will post from those accounts to give the impression that there are many people who agree with their positions. Don't fall for this trick. Do not feed the trolls.

# Problem 8: Forgetting the social part of social media

Social media isn't just about posting links that interest you or talking about things that interest you. It's about being social – talking with people, connecting, having real conversations. If you're on Twitter and you approach a business with a question about their services, it's much better if they give you a human response to your question instead of a link to a pre-written media release.

Social media is a great way to keep tabs on the people in your life. You might not see your old friends who have moved away to another part of the country, but with

**West Kent Book Club**

Home    Members    Sponsors    Photos    Pages    Discussions ▾    Money    More ▾      Join us!

Dartford, United Kingdom
Founded Jan 11, 2009

Read more about us...

| | |
|---|---|
| Book Readers | 75 |
| Group reviews | 8 |
| Upcoming Meetups | 5 |
| Past Meetups | 42 |

Our calendar

Membership dues
GBP2.00 for each meeting

Organizers:
Lisa, anna and 2 more...
View The Leadership Team

Only Organizers can add Meetups

Contact us

## July Book Group = The Finkler Question by Howard Jacobsen

📅 **Saturday, July 30, 2011, 10:30 AM**
SELECTED BY: LISA

📍 **Dartford Library**
Dartford Park, Dartford (map)
SELECTED BY: LISA

💷 **Price:** GBP2.00/per person
Refund policy

'He should have seen it coming. His life had been one mishap after another. So he should have been prepared for this one...'

Julian Treslove, a professionally unspectacular former BBC radio producer, and Sam Finkler, a popular Jewish philosopher, writer and television personality, are old school friends. Despite a prickly relationship and very different lives, they've never quite lost touch with each other - or with their former teacher, Libor Sevcik, a Czech always more concerned with the wider world than with exam results.

Now, both Libor and Sam are recently widowed, and with Treslove, his chequered and unsuccessful record with women rendering him an honorary third widower, they dine at Libor's grand, central London apartment.

It's a sweetly painful evening of reminiscence in which all three remove themselves to a time before they had loved and lost; a time before they had

**11 attending**
RSVPS CLOSED

EVENT HOST
**Lisa**
ORGANIZER

**Kate Withstandley**
My mum is coming too, hope this is ok, she hasn't got round to confirming online yet...

**julie**

**Esther**
no photo yet

**Christine King**
This will be my first meeting with you all and i think im looking forward to it. Hope ill fit

Facebook (for example) you can see when their kids are sick, when they've enjoyed themselves on a holiday, or when they've been promoted at work or run a marathon. It's always good to comment on things they post, reply to them on Twitter or give them an occasional like.

Not that you're trying to endear yourself to them, of course, but social media makes it easy to keep alive your connections with many people.

How to keep connected in real life?

**1** Don't assume that just because you're friends with someone on Facebook, you are now deeply connected. You might see that they've posted this or that message about their life, but do you really know what's going on? Pick up the phone, invite them out to lunch, and talk. Maybe they're not feeling good about their job security, or they have a sick family member.

**2** Use social media to create gatherings of friends and colleagues. For example, if you have a birthday coming up, why not create a birthday celebration at your favourite pub and then invite Facebook friends to drop by? Or why not create a lunch gathering for your local business group using Twitter?

▶ **SEE ALSO:** Want to know more about social gatherings near you? Check out http://www.meetup.com, http://www.tweetvite.com and similar sites.

# Problem 9: Getting distracted by too much social media

I know people who have accounts on every single social media service you can imagine. They literally spend hours each day updating information, conversing with people, uploading photos and writing blog posts. Social media has become their full-time vocation.

This may work for them, but I'm willing to bet that it won't for you. My advice? Find a maximum of three things you're willing to spend some time on and make those three your focus. For example, you might join Facebook for personal sharing, use Flickr to share your love of photography and use Tumblr to blog about your travels.

Having accounts on these three services will keep you very busy but won't make people totally sick of you and your constant social media updates. Later on you can add more services if you like, or decide to drop one in favour of another.

The best way to handle social media overload?

1 Remember that most social media is a stream of messages that goes by. It's not like your email inbox where you have to handle each message. Most of those tweets and Facebook updates don't have anything to do with you.

2 I try to focus mostly on any messages that have been sent directly to me. For example, anyone sending a public tweet or direct message to @myerman gets my attention first. Same goes for Facebook or Google+.

3 After responding to any requests made directly to me, I might sample to see what my closest friends and family are doing and saying.

4 I then might spend some time on my favourite blogs.

5 Then and only then do I worry about what total strangers are saying out on Twitter, for example. In other words, I give most of my focus to people who interact directly with me and who are in my social circles.

# Problem 10: Not participating enough in social media

The opposite problem of the person who is overcommitted to social media is the person who hardly ever does anything with their account. They sign up for Twitter but only tweet every three months or so, and it's always something banal. They sign up for Facebook but only lurk and never post. They set up a blog but write only once a year.

If you're not going to be somewhat active on social media, then there's no point in signing up for any of the services. The fact that you're on the service will attract the attention of your friends, who will be happy to connect with you – so get active! If you can't get excited about the services you are using, maybe try to find something else.

I've met many people who were blogging because it was 'the thing to do' but who were miserable bloggers, but who flourished when they discovered their love of making and posting videos to YouTube (for example).

Best ways to remain active on social media?

1. Get involved with people who share your interests or points of view. If you're a knitter, find knitting groups on Facebook, go to events where knitters get together, and get social in real life. Your social media time will be enriched because you will know these people.

2. Set aside a little bit of time every day to check up on people. It doesn't have to be a lot of time, just 15 minutes a day. Check in, write a few notes, respond to people, say hello, leave a few comments. Eventually, people will start interacting back and you'll start having fun.

3. If a social media outlet isn't working for you, then don't be afraid to quit it. If Twitter is more fun than Facebook, then don't feel bad that you're spending more time on Twitter.

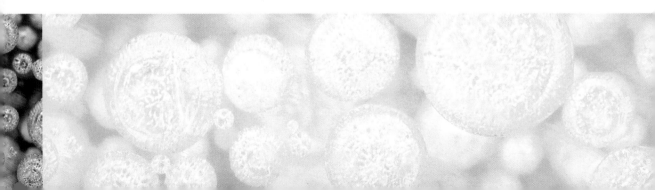

# Also available in the In Simple Steps series

9780273761099

9780273745419

9780273771296

9780273744146

9780273729181

9780273734932

9780273762591

9780273729129

9780273729174

9780273761105

9780273761082

9780273746355

in Simple steps